DOGS

everything you need to know to care for your pet

Written by
Heather Latimer

Edited by
Susan Lurie

Illustrated by
Bill Kresse

PRESTIGE BOOKS, INC.
New York, New York

Designed by Irva Mandelbaum

Contents

Choosing Your Dog

- **The Best Age to Obtain a Puppy**
- **Selecting a Male**
- **Selecting a Female**
- **Mixed Breeds vs. Purebreeds**
- **Where to Buy a Dog**
- **Selecting a Puppy from a Litter**
- **How to Make Sure Your New Pet Is Healthy**
- **Your Pet's Personality**
- **Superior Swimmers**
- **Climate Considerations**
- **Apartment Pets**
- **House Pets**
- **Dogs for Infants, the Elderly, and the Handicapped**
- **A Breed for People Who Are Allergic to Dogs**
- **Registering Purebreeds with the American Kennel Club**

How old should your puppy be when you select him?

Kennel owners like to sell 6- to 8-week-old pups. They make the most profit then because the puppy, in their care for so short a time, has cost very little to maintain. However, if you are buying the pup from a kennel, it is recommended that you buy a 10- to 12-week-old pup. He may be as old as six months when obtained if he has had loving care from a kennel or family. But remember, when his formative weeks have been spent in the company of other animals with little personal attention, he could be difficult to handle. A puppy who is accustomed to the human touch will make a better pet.

Should you choose a dog or a bitch?

Many people favor a bitch because she is often quieter and more conservative than her male counterpart. She is also considered cleaner and easier to train, but some people are wary about her "heat" period, a time when she is capable of conceiving and is particularly popular with the males of her species. However, this problem can be solved by having her spayed. Other people enjoy the outgoing behavior exhibited by the male, even though he does have a tendency to get into fights with other dogs and wander away from home in search of sexual adventure.

When looking for a pup, how do you recognize symptoms of ill-health?

Indications that all is not well include a running nose; excessive mucous discharge from the eyes; white spots or a blue-grey cast to the eyes; a bloated stomach when the rest of the body is slender; protruding ribs or hip bones; fur that is not shiny if the dog is smooth-coated; sparse fur with mangy patches; dry, scaly, or sore skin; trembling or listlessness. Diarrhea or vomiting may be either temporary or a sign of serious internal disorders. The dog's temperature should be approximately 101.5°F., although up to 102°F. is normal. His nose—hot or cold, wet or dry—has nothing to do with his health, in spite of what many people believe.

What is the best breed for you?

When you select your pet, think about the size of your house, the climate where you live, and whether or not neighbors are close enough to be

bothered by barking. Also keep in mind the dog's temperament. Will it fit in with your lifestyle? Will the dog be living with youngsters or elderly people? Consider how much time you have to exercise a large hound and the space available for him to run on your property. Do you or your family have the time to devote to some breeds which need hours of daily brushing or frequent bathing or the money for those breeds that need frequent salon grooming? Read the breed guides for characteristics of each type.

It seems that purebreeds today are different in size and shape than those of the past. Have they changed physically?

Indeed they have! Some differences have come about naturally as a result of their activities and environment; others are due to careful breeding methods by professionals. Some purebreeds are now taller, have longer legs, or are smaller than in bygone days.

Are mongrels—mixed breeds or dogs of uncertain origin—friendlier than purebreeds?

We can be certain of the characteristics to expect in a purebreed because they are outlined in breed directories, but mongrels have unpredictable qualities. However, they are often extremely endearing. On the other hand, their doubtful lineage could make them disagreeable. When you select a mixed breed, you are taking a chance, but if you don't gamble, you might miss out on a rewarding pet.

What is a mutt?

A mutt is the result of breeding many different types of dogs, all or most of whom are of unknown ancestry. The mutt is sometimes called a mongrel, a Heinz dog (after the food manufacturer of 57 varieties), or mixed breed. If you have taken a fancy to the dog and decide to buy him, you can be proud that you own the only dog of his exact makeup anywhere in the world.

Is there any financial reason to select a mutt over a purebreed?

Food and care for both types of dogs are usually the same. However, the initial cost is considerably more for a specific breed than for a mutt. Also, you may want fancy grooming for the pet of pure strain, and that means spending more money. When it comes to food, the size of the mature dog is a significant factor since a toy eats less than 1/2 pound of food per day while a mixed Wolfhound gulps down 5 pounds. Try to estimate the size of the dog when fully grown. He will probably resemble his mother. If she is not available, check his paws. Big paws are a sure sign of a large dog to come.

Are toy breeds or miniatures more delicate than larger dogs?

Not necessarily. They can be just as robust and healthy as larger dogs, but their owners tend to pamper them, encouraging the development of finicky natures. Other people go to opposite extremes and put their toys through harrowing experiences. Don't spoil your pet by carrying him everywhere, but don't walk him in crowds without a leash either. If he can't keep up with his master, he could drown in a sea of shoes, and this kind of experience could instigate nervous disorders, or early heart attacks, or even result in your pet's untimely death. A small breed should walk along uncrowded paths, and he should be picked up when there are many pedestrians about.

How can you be sure your puppy will have a good temperament when he grows up?

Buy one that is six months old, for his personality will be apparent by then. Look for a curious, playful, and affectionate pup, and stay away from those who snarl, growl, and viciously snap (as opposed to light-hearted nips).

Do you want a dog who can perform tricks?

The Miniature or Standard Poodle is a natural clown and, due to his superior intelligence, can often be trained to be a great performer. Some, without instruction, can dance on their hind legs.

People say you should never purchase a dog from a pet shop. Why?

It depends upon the pet shop and where the owner buys his animals. Does the owner keep his shop clean? Are the animals and their cages well kept? Even if the answer is "yes" to these questions, many, many people frequent pet shops, allowing one dog after another to lick their germ-covered fingers. Some pet shop owners purchase their stock from reputable local breeders, while others buy animals who have been bred on puppy farms. The latter are usually shipped by air in packed crates passed through numerous hands, and subjected to many fearful experiences. But there are alert, healthy, adorable animals in pet stores. You must judge the owner, his premises, and the pet on an individual basis.

Newspapers carry many notices offering free pups. Is it wise to answer these advertisements?

By all means, look at the litter. If the one you like appears healthy and clean, inspect the mother and father. Are they big or small? Remember, the pup's adult size will bear some relationship to that of his parents. Ask what the pup has been fed to determine if his diet has been adequate. Has the pet been wormed and inoculated? If so, when and by whom? Make sure you can return the pet in case he is ill. Then rush to the vet and have the dog examined before you become too attached to him.

If you acquire a mature dog, is there a chance that he might not understand English?

Yes. On a trans-Atlantic ship's "Pooch Promenade," I saw an American exercising a beautiful hound. A fellow passenger accused him of showing off by talking to the animal in German, but he quickly explained that he had received the dog while on military duty in Bonn and the canine simply did not understand English. Meanwhile, a nearby Welshman was training a baby Cocker Spaniel to respond to commands in Gaelic, a couple were issuing orders to their pet in Swedish, an Argentinian was having his say in Spanish, and a Parisian and her dog were communicating in French. Keep in mind the possibility that a mature dog coming from a large city, a place where people speak diverse languages, might not understand English.

Should you go to a humane society or an animal pound when you want to buy a dog?

Certainly. Many animal adoption societies take great care of their animals. Often, a veterinarian checks the boarders every day and the sick ones are properly treated. By all means, do consider providing a home for a dog whose days would otherwise be numbered, for a good deal of shelters lack facilities and funds to keep animals for an extended period of time. (They are put to sleep if no one claims them.) Avoid amateur owners who collect countless strays, house them in cramped quarters, and pay little attention to them. These dogs are usually infested with fleas, worms, and other parasites, and are not physically sound.

Once decided on the breed you want, where do you find the breeder?

The national publication *Dog World* may be helpful, or ask your local veterinarian for information on a new litter from a reliable breeder. A listing of breeders is available from the American Kennel Club (AKC), 51 Madison Avenue, New York, New York 10010. Visiting a dog show is a good idea, but first read up on the breed of your choice so you know what characteristics to look for, especially if you have hopes of showing or breeding the dog. Above all, don't be swayed by the enthusiasm of a breeder whose litter is not of the highest standard.

Why don't some breeders permit people to look at the animals too closely?

Don't be dismayed if the breeder does not allow you to get too close to the litter. People going from kennel to kennel in search of a pup can carry germs on their hands or clothing, and breeders know that people let dogs lick their fingers. The breeders asking you to keep some distance from the pups are probably concerned about the health of their litter.

You want to choose a puppy from a litter. How can you tell them apart? Which one do you select?

When they are all spirited and winsome, your problem is understandable. Use the process of elimination. For instance, if you want a male, have all the females removed. Now study the remaining pups. Does one look sickly? Have him taken out. Reject the one whose ears do not stand up as perkily as the rest, and so on. You still can't decide between two? Pick the one who appears most affectionate or most independent. Once you've narrowed down your choice to one, ask the owner to trim the whiskers from both sides of the pup's muzzle so you can identify him when it's time to take him home.

What does the term "runt of the litter" mean?

The runt of the litter is the smallest member of the group and is usually not in top physical condition. Therefore, he may be less expensive than his brothers and sisters. There is a chance that, once removed from the larger animals in the litter, the runt will grow to be a strong, healthy dog. But be cautious, this is not probable.

Is it true that the coats of certain breeds change in color?

Only a few breeds drastically change color. A silver Poodle is born black, the color turning silver around his nose when he's about six weeks old, gradually extending over the entire coat. Kerry Blue Terriers are also born black but grow paler. Most dogs who have coats of dark brown, rich red, apricot, and cream tend to lighten in shade as they age. And a Dalmatian, which is born pure white, acquires his trademark spots three or four weeks later.

There is a great demand for well-bred German Shepherds. Where can you find one?

German Shepherds are being snapped up as watchdogs, guard dogs, and guide dogs for the sightless. Reputable breeders often have waiting lists, and some people are hastily producing poor specimens (even under the best conditions, German Shepherds are subject to diarrhea and hip dysplasia—a malformation of the hip socket and the leg that fits into it). There are many other large, bold, and protective animals worth considering. The Giant Schnauzer, for instance, would make a very alert watchdog, and the Belgian Sheepdog learns quickly and is a guard dog by nature.

Should you give your child a puppy for Christmas?

A pet is not a toy. If he is handled too much, his health and growth will suffer. Picking him up, putting him down, awakening him from sleep—all this unending devotion could destroy your new puppy. So make sure he receives proper care and attention.

Are any breeds considered superior swimmers? Can they be trusted water companions for children?

American Water Spaniels, Irish Water Spaniels, Otter Hounds, Chesapeake Bay Retrievers, Labrador Retrievers, and Newfoundlands are breeds that are recognized for their ability to swim well, and they are gentle and trustworthy companions for children.

What breeds are comfortable in hot climates?

The Italian Greyhound, Whippet, Dachshund, German Shorthaired Pointer, Dalmatian, and Smooth-haired Fox Terrier are all at ease in warmer areas. The Pekinese and English or French Bulldog, however, suffer from severe respiratory difficulties in intense heat and high altitudes. Also, if you live in a hot-weather region, do not select an animal with a long or heavy coat like an Old English Sheepdog or Afghan Hound.

What breeds can withstand very cold, Alaska-like winters?

Saint Bernard, Siberian Husky, Alaskan Malamute, Eskimo, Samoyed, Newfoundland, Norwegian Elkhound—these large dogs all enjoy and thrive in icy weather.

Is there a dog capable of catching rats?

The Terrier breeds sometimes prove to be eager rat killers.

What kind of dog would be a suitable apartment pet?

The Basenji of Africa, also called the "barkless dog," would be perfect for an apartment. (In fact, he does make a little noise that sounds like yodeling.) A mixed-breed Poodle, such as the Cockapoo, is also a fine alternative, for he is not as high strung as his purebred ancestors. In general, an apartment pet should be small if you have limited space and relatively quiet so he does not disturb the neighbors.

You have a large house with plenty of land, and you would like a dog. What breed do you select?

With such expansive grounds, you can choose any type of dog you desire. A large one, perhaps a Labrador Retriever, Golden Retriever, Boxer, Great Dane, Old English Sheepdog (if you don't mind grooming him every day), or Collie would be ideal; these breeds love to run and romp.

Should you obtain a dog suffering from monorchidism?

Monorchidism is a hereditary defect in a male dog—he has one testicle that has not descended into the scrotum. This dog is not suitable either for breeding or showing, even if the condition is surgically corrected. But he will have all the characteristics of a Champion, according to his background and breeding, and would probably make a fine pet.

16

Are two dogs better than one?

If you have the space and can afford two dogs, yes. It is great for a dog to have his own canine companion. Try to get them both at the same time, or introduce the second while the first is still young, so they can easily adjust to each other's presence. Don't bring a pup into a house with an aging animal, for the older dog will become agitated.

Is a dog a good companion for an elderly person?

Older people often outlive their friends and become very lonely. A lively canine could be a joyous companion, but an aged person should not be saddled with a pup who needs housebreaking and training. Get a grown, housebroken mongrel or pedigreed dog from a reputable animal pound, and insist upon a guarantee that he may be returned within a specified period if desired.

Do *all* blind people need guide dogs? Where do you get a guide dog?

Out of approximately 450,000 legally blind men and women in the United States, only 2% can be helped by a guide dog. Some people are too young; others are not flexible enough or are too old to adapt. Lack of hearing, poor physical condition, or mental incapacity may disqualify someone from owning a guide dog. And there are those who have sufficient sight to get around by themselves or are more adept with a cane. Contact The Seeing Eye, Morristown, New Jersey, to receive more information. If a blind person is accepted into the training program, he must pay $150, which covers transportation to and from The Seeing Eye center, one month of lessons in using the dog, room and board during the month spent at the school, the dog, his training, and a special harness and other equipment. Guide dogs are usually scientifically bred and have received three months of training.

Can a handicapped person have a dog?

Of course. However, the dog must be gentle and unlikely to overpower the handicapped owner, and the owner must be capable of feeding and exercising the animal. Often, a large, gentle breed, such as a Greyhound, can be trained to walk slowly and close to his master, who can then place a hand on the dog's back and use him for support. A mature pet (rather than an exuberant puppy) adopted from a humane society is recommended. The dog should be female—a male dog may race off after a female, forgetting his duty to his handicapped owner.

Can a middle-aged couple give a dog a suitable home?

Yes. But if you have a yen to travel, the dog will become a problem, and you'll either find yourself giving up trips or spending a great deal of money on boarding kennels.

What dog should you choose if you have a baby in the house?

A *grown* dog who has been known to treat little children tenderly is the best choice. Ask your local humane association for one that is placid, gentle, and protective, and comes from a home where there were small children. A young pup is not an appropriate friend for a baby, for he has sharp teeth and may accidentally scrape the baby's delicate skin. Any dog, during affectionate play, can topple a toddler, so always keep a watchful eye when the two are together. And, if you do buy a puppy, remember, he may grow faster than the baby, so wait until the child is at least four years old.

Is there a dog for people who are allergic to fur?

Try the Mexican Hairless. Although his lack of fur may at first be disturbing, his peppy personality will soon win you over. When happy, he is playful and loving, and if upset, he weeps real tears. There are many different colors, from pink to black, but the black one doesn't seem so bare. The male grows slightly larger than the female, about 12 inches in height and 15 pounds in weight.

Does it matter whether or not you register your purebreed with the American Kennel Club (AKC)?

It is not necessary if your dog is simply your companion. However, if you want to enter him in shows or breed him to a purebred bitch (in the latter case, you would be rewarded with a stud fee or one of the resulting puppies), he must be registered. If your purebreed is not registered, none of his descendants will ever be eligible for AKC registration. This means that he and his offspring will have little monetary value, and his family tree will cease to be of any consequence, no matter how distinguished it is.

Where can you obtain a complete pedigree of your purebred dog?

If the breeder does not supply it, write the AKC. Request a three-generation or four-generation pedigree. The longer genealogy costs more but it's worth the price to have proof of your pet's long-distinguished ancestry. You will probably receive the pedigree from the AKC within three to four weeks.

What papers should you receive with the purchase of a pedigreed animal?

• Certificate of registration or an application form for this certificate. The breeder must sign these forms in the appropriate place.

• Record of inoculation for distemper, leptospirosis, and hepatitis, stating the date of each inoculation, what vaccine was given, and the date the vaccinations should be repeated.

• Certification that the parents of the pup were judged free of hip dysplasia. (This certification is especially important for German Shepherds and large breeds—they run a high risk of inheriting this malformation.)

• Information regarding date of worming and the type of worms found (if any).

• Instructions for care, training, and a feeding schedule.

He's Yours Now

- **Naming Your Pet**
- **Paper Training**
- **Indoor Mischief!**
- **The Shy Puppy**
- **Outdoor Training**
- **Sleeping with Your Dog**
- **Collars and Leashes**
- **Going Out for a Walk**
- **Jogging with Your Dog**
- **Lifting Your Pet**
- **The Dog's Wardrobe**
- **Spaying or Neutering Your Pet**

Can you give a dog a name he will like?

Choose several names. Then, speaking very slowly, call the dog by each. Some he will ignore, but at the sound of others, his ears will prick up, or he may cock his head to the side. From those he responds to, select one, and use it for the rest of his life.

How do you teach the dog to answer to his name?

For best results, use his name under pleasant circumstances. Say it when announcing mealtime even though he's right at your elbow, nudging you to fill his bowl quickly. Always use the dog's name when calling him to come, but never use it when scolding him or issuing the command "Stay."

The AKC has strict rules regarding names that may be registered. True or False?

True. The name you submit must not contain more than twenty-five letters, and it must be accompanied by a second choice in case the first has already been taken. It must not be indecent or downgrading to the dog, and it cannot be the same name of any living dignitary or celebrity. You do not have to call the dog by the name given to the AKC—one Miniature Poodle, registered as "Celeste of the Range," answered to "Frisky." Often, the breeder has filed for each member of the litter prior to your purchase. (He does this to ensure that the kennel's name is included on the form.) So, before you register your dog's name, check to see if the breeder has already done it.

What is "paper training"?

It is teaching your pup to relieve himself on newspapers spread out on the floor. To be effective, confine him to an area that is completely covered with newspaper. Gradually, reduce the size of this area until only a small newspaper-covered spot remains. To maintain a permanent place in your home for his lifetime use, make a pad consisting of one sheet of newspaper for every 2 pounds of your animal's weight. For instance, if your dog weighs 20 pounds, your pad will contain ten sheets of paper. Now, all you have to do is remove the top sheets when they become soiled, adding clean sheets *underneath*.

What can you do for the paper-trained dog with inaccurate aim?

Accompany him to the newspaper and nudge him until all four paws are on the covered area. However, make sure there is enough newspaper to accommodate the size of your dog. If not, spread out some more.

Dog's Weight	Newspaper Size
Under 8 pounds	11" X 14"
9 – 15 pounds	14" X 22"
16 – 35 pounds	23" X 29"
36 – 60 pounds	29" X 29"
61 – 135 pounds	46" X 46"

How many times a day will your dog "go to the bathroom"?

For a pup: upon awakening, after daytime naps, before eating, before drinking, after eating, after drinking, after playing, before going to bed, during the night, and/or every half hour. As he grows, his "bathroom visits" will be less frequent. For an adult: upon awakening, after eating and drinking, before going to bed, and/or every 2 1/2 to 3 hours. Never withhold water from your pup because you think it will keep him from urinating frequently. Also bear in mind that if you fill your dog's dish with food on a regular basis, he will eliminate regularly too.

Is there any way you can tell that a dog is about to urinate or defecate?

Yes. Males and females are likely to turn in circles several times. A female, a young male, or a neutered male may begin to squat, and a mature male will start to lift his leg.

Your dog doesn't lift his leg when he urinates. Is this normal?

Leg-lifting is innate and usually starts at puberty, about six months of age. However, many males develop the habit much later. Neutered dogs often continue to squat throughout their lives.

Will it take a long time to teach your dog not to defecate in the house?

A three-month-old puppy will usually respond to training after about two weeks. If he does not, it may be the owner's fault. Patience, consistency, and understanding are the keys to success. Let the pup know which acts please you and which ones offend, for he will do his best to earn your praises. And be fair: don't punish the dog if you left him alone too long with no place to relieve himself, or if you didn't understand his request to be let outdoors.

Should you rub your dog's nose in the mess he makes?

This old-fashioned idea is dangerous. Your pet's nostrils can become infected, and he might swallow some feces. Watch him instead, and if he relieves himself in the wrong place, whack his rump with a rolled up newspaper and say, in an angry tone, "B-a-d, b-a-d." Then take him to the proper spot and leave him there. Having just eliminated, he may not use the approved site immediately, but in time he will understand what is expected of him.

Your pup gets so excited when you return home from an outing that he wets the floor. Can you do something to prevent this?

Not really. He's so happy to see you, he loses control. As his muscles grow stronger, he'll overcome this, but in the meantime, don't punish him—feeling happy and fearful at the same time, he will become confused.

If the dog vomits or urinates on your carpet, is there any way to remove the stains?

Clean the mess immediately. First, wipe up the excess fluid with paper towels. Then saturate the spot with club soda, allowing it to soak into the stain for about three minutes. Blot the area and repeat this procedure. When the stain has been lifted, using paper towels, dry the carpet thoroughly. If you have a hair dryer or an electric heater, dry the spot again because a carpet that remains damp may rot.

Your puppy behaves downstairs, but now that he has learned to climb the steps, he relieves himself upstairs. What do you do?

He doesn't understand the same rules apply to different parts of the house or in your friends' homes either. So follow him, watch his antics during these new explorations, and if you see him preparing to relieve himself, rush him to the appropriate indoor or outdoor location. After a few of these unexpected, hasty trips, he will get the message.

Should you allow your dog to relieve himself indoors on some occasions even though he is trained to go outdoors?

Yes. Retain the indoor facility for his use during the night or when you are not home. He need never be trained to go outside if it is inconvenient for you.

When you let the dog out to urinate, he races back inside. Why?

Your dog doesn't understand why he has been let out. He probably thinks he is being punished or you do not love him anymore, and he rushes back to make amends. Next time, accompany him outside. Place a piece of newspaper on which he has previously urinated (it need not be wet) on the spot you would like him to use. When he performs, praise him lavishly. Repeat the procedure until he understands what is expected and no longer needs the newspaper as a reminder.

Is it true that dogs like to return to the same spot to relieve themselves?

Yes. And it is usually your favorite shrub. If you want to discourage the use of a certain area, sprinkle it with pepper. It will not harm the dog's nose, and the memory of the smell will keep him away long after the pepper is gone. When a new dog moves into the neighborhood, sprinkle with pepper again. If you approve of the site your dog has chosen, all you have to do is make sure he reaches it in time.

Why does your pup cry every night?

He is just a baby and accustomed to snuggling up to relatives of his own kind. Now he's alone, he misses them and the warmth of their bodies. To compensate for these losses, let him sleep near you in a warm, cozy bed. To make a mattress for him, fill a rubber water bottle with lukewarm water and cover it with a blanket. Then, place another blanket (a soft one) over him and put a ticking clock nearby—to simulate his mother's heartbeat—or a radio playing quiet music, and he won't be so lonely.

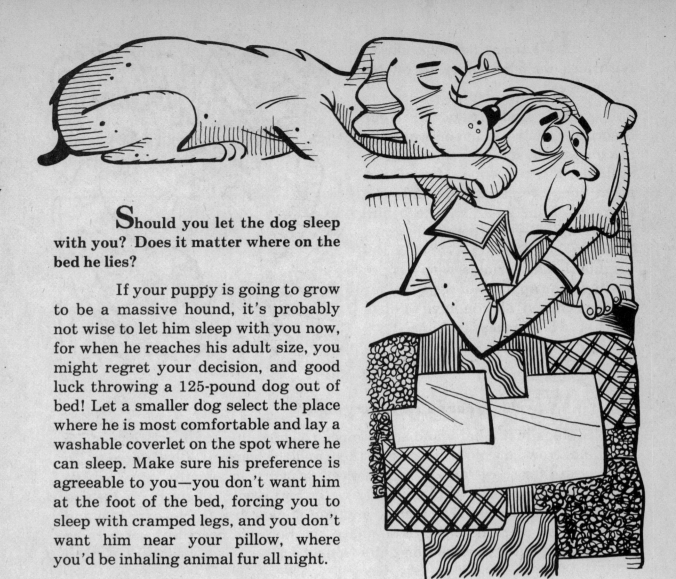

Should you let the dog sleep with you? Does it matter where on the bed he lies?

If your puppy is going to grow to be a massive hound, it's probably not wise to let him sleep with you now, for when he reaches his adult size, you might regret your decision, and good luck throwing a 125-pound dog out of bed! Let a smaller dog select the place where he is most comfortable and lay a washable coverlet on the spot where he can sleep. Make sure his preference is agreeable to you—you don't want him at the foot of the bed, forcing you to sleep with cramped legs, and you don't want him near your pillow, where you'd be inhaling animal fur all night.

The puppy is terribly shy and afraid of his new home. Will he overcome this fear?

Your living room appears vast to one so tiny; his only experience has been sharing small quarters with his mother and siblings. Construct an enclosed area for him where he will feel safe and secure, or better still, use a baby's playpen—it comes with a waterproof base. (Restricting him has many benefits: he can't roam when you're absent during the day or asleep at night, or get underfoot when you are busily moving about.) After he's adjusted to this small range, he will grow more bold, slowly searching out new territory each day. Recognizing the pen as his special place, he will return to it regularly. Make sure it is substantially larger than, and far from, his bed, especially if he is not toilet trained. Confined much of the time, he will probably relieve himself in the pen, and if the pen resembles the bed, he might think it's proper to do it there too. (Generally, however, pets have an inborn instinct not to soil their sleeping area.)

When the family is home, the puppy hides under the table, but left with one person, he frolics freely. Why? What can you do about it?

Surrounded by many people twenty times his size frightens him. Be subtle: don't try to grab him. Move away from the table, play ball with one another, drop a biscuit on the rug, put down a saucer of milk, talk to each other, listen to soothing music. Soon he will reappear to join in the activities.

Why does the dog tremble and cower at the sight of someone nearing?

Most likely, the dog has been mistreated by his former owner and needs gentle handling and constant affection. Avoid raising your voice, do not make sudden moves, and postpone obedience training that is not absolutely necessary. In time, you will win his confidence, and he will forget past terrors.

The puppy chewed your new straw hat—and you thought only goats did this. Why did he do it?

When he's teething, your puppy will nibble on anything, and indeed, he should have something to gnaw on to ease his discomfort. So, give him items that are made for this purpose: a genuine leather ball, artificial bones, real bones that will not splinter (no wooden or plastic objects, hollow toys, or toys containing noisemakers). Don't tempt him by leaving your belongings in reach, and, if you go out, leave him in a room where there is nothing he can destroy—the kitchen or bathroom are possibilities, once towels and other chewable articles have been removed.

He had a good appetite while he was with his litter, but now he's home, and he won't eat. What's wrong?

It could be that he's excited and not ready to settle down to eat, or he may not like his new diet. But, most likely, he is unhappy dining without the company of his brothers and sisters. If there is no reason to suspect he is sick, consider this a phase, a temporary reaction to his new environment. Also, make sure the food is not too tough—he might need his meal in the form of mash—and cut into small pieces.

Will a bitch become emotionally disturbed or die young if she is not permitted to mate or have a litter?

It is not necessary for her to engage in sexual activities or become a mother in order to have a long and happy life. She will live just as long, or even longer, if she does not bear litters.

What happens when the female goes into "heat"?

Prior to onset, her external sexual organs appear bloated. Then, a discharge follows, which is colorless, but gradually changes to pink or red during the course of the first few days. This condition, called *estrus*, lasts from eighteen to twenty-one days and occurs regularly every six, seven, or eight months, depending on the individual bitch. Estrus, usually starting sometime after the age of seven months but before fourteen months, is the only time your female can conceive.

Must you spay your female pedigreed pup?

You should, unless you wish to breed or exhibit her in shows. The advantages of spaying are many: you won't have to worry about unwanted litters, she will not need to be confined during heat periods, she will not develop tumors in the breast or female organs.

At what age should the female be spayed? Will it make her fat?

Opinions vary, but many people agree that it is best to hold off spaying until after the first heat period. Spaying will not cause her to become sluggish or fat, provided she gets plenty of fresh air and exercise and is fed a balanced diet—no scraps or cookies!

Why is it so expensive to have a bitch spayed?

Spaying is a very delicate operation and requires skill and great precision. It is somewhat like a woman's hysterectomy, but since it is performed on comparatively minute organs, it becomes a far more difficult procedure.

Are there any less expensive places people can take their pets to be spayed?

Yes. Many large animal institutions offer special low-cost spaying programs during the year. Sometimes community leaders open temporary centers for those who can't afford to take their animals to a private veterinarian. Local vets, as a contribution to the community, may also offer this service free of charge or for a fee as low as five dollars.

What happens when a dog is castrated?

This process is also called *neutering*. The veterinarian removes the sperm-producing contents of the testicles, and the animal is no longer fertile. The anesthetized pet doesn't feel any pain during surgery. (Neutering is not as complicated as spaying and, therefore, costs less.) The procedure can be performed around the age of six months and any time after. Although many people cringe at the thought, neutering is in the best interests of the owner and the neighborhood in which he lives, unless, of course, the dog is to be used for breeding. The animal's personality will be relatively unchanged: he will not be driven with the desire to mate and, thus, will be less restless, no longer straying in search of sexual encounters. This operation is not suggested for guard dogs, for it might tame their aggressive natures.

Should you pick up your puppy by the scruff of the neck?

The mother does, carrying the pup in her teeth, but the pup is close to her body and not very high above the ground. When a child or an adult attempts it, the dog is hoisted into space and becomes terrified. So tenderly place one hand under his chest, the other under his hindquarters, and lift him gently into your arms, holding him close to your body.

How do you lift a big dog?

Bend to the dog's level, enclose his four legs in your arms, and raise him as you straighten up. Since you might strain yourself, don't do it unnecessarily.

When does the collar go on?

Put a collar on your pup when he's about twelve weeks old because he needs plenty of time to adjust to it before a leash is attached. He may shake his head a bit or try to paw it off. If he strongly objects, let him wear it for a few hours each day, pretending it is a special treat. A narrow, genuine leather collar is best, and if it has studs, make sure they do not dig into his neck or, better still, that the collar is lined. Once he wears it permanently, he'll be ready to train to walk with a leash. (Leash training is done in the home.) It is vital to check the dog's growth each week, refitting the collar so it does not choke him. Remove it occasionally to give his neck a brisk rub and to brush the flattened fur.

What identification should a dog wear on his collar?

Without identification your pet can readily be picked up by any local animal control authority and impounded, or taken home by a stranger who believes he is a stray. The collar should have the following attached to it: license tag, rabies tag, and tag or plate bearing your name, address, and telephone number. Your dog's collar should *not* contain his name, for this allows strangers to call him by name, making it easier to lure him away.

What kind of leash is best?

It is a matter of preference. A leather leash must be examined periodically to make sure the dog has not chewed it to the snapping point. Also see that it hasn't dried out, ready to disintegrate. Some people like chains because a good one won't come apart, but a dog on a chain might look more like a prisoner than man's "best friend."

Should you use a harness instead of a leash?

There is no advantage in using a harness in place of a leash. In fact, some owners believe it may ruin the dog's shoulders, make his elbows protrude, and give him bowlegs. If you decide on a harness, alternate its use with a leash to prevent the dog's fur from getting worn in a single area.

Will a pup easily adapt to a leash attached to his collar?

Not always. If he is reluctant, take the following steps: 1. Put his leash on and let him walk around the house, dragging it behind. However, you must watch him. The leash can become entangled with telephone wires or electrical cords, or encircle an object, causing it to fall on him. If this happens, he'll be petrified of the leash, and, of course, he might get hurt. 2. Once the pup seems comfortable, pick up the leash by the loop and follow him, allowing for a slight pull on the collar as he moves. Do not attempt to control his movements unless he is in danger. 3. Next, coax him to follow *you*, as you trot about the room. If he balks or fights the leash, lure him with a tidbit, carrying something he likes to eat in your hand so he keeps pace—the smell of the food might draw him forward—and offer it to him as a reward. 4. If all this fails, have someone else hold the leash a short distance away. Call the pup. He may dash toward you, so tell your friend not to drop the leash but to be ready to follow quickly. After repeating this a few times, take the leash yourself and start again from step 2.

How old does your puppy have to be for his first walk in the street?

Do not take him walking in germ-ridden streets until he has completed all his shots and/or is six months of age. (All his leash training should have taken place within the home or on your own property.) As an introduction, carry him into busy shopping centers the first few times he goes out so he gradually adapts to strange odors, noises, and crowds.

What do you do when your pup sits down and refuses to budge on his walk?

The bustling pedestrians and traffic noises are probably making him nervous. Be compassionate and try this: carry him on the outward journey. When it's time to go home, put him down. You'll be amazed to find that he will hurry all the way back without any coaxing.

Your dog hangs around the table at mealtime, begging for food. How can you break him of this habit?

Never feed your dog scraps from the table. But if the habit has been established, ask diners not to feed the dog directly. After the meal is over, give your dog a plate of tidbits as a reward for sitting quietly.

Does a dog need clothing?

A practical dog jacket and waterproof boots are acceptable in bad weather, but don't dress him in people clothes. He is neither a child nor a toy and deserves to be treated with dignity and respect.

Is playing "Tug o' War" with your puppy bad for his teeth?

Although it seems like lots of fun, it can have serious consequences. Teaching your pet roughhouse tactics is no good for his teeth, and it is even worse for his disposition. Once he realizes you cannot get anything away from him when he clenches his powerful teeth, he may be on his way to becoming a dangerous weapon instead of a devoted pet.

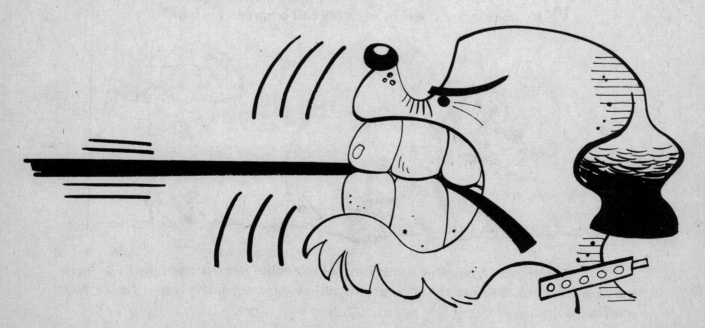

How can you keep the dog off fine upholstered furniture?

The dog settles himself in your chair because he thinks he is a person too. It would be nice to allow him to use one specific chair, but if this is not possible, provide him with a special place on the floor—perhaps on a nice comfortable rug or blanket—where there are no drafts. You've done this and he still returns to the furniture? Then, each time he defies you, push him off and scold him in a rougher tone of voice.

Your clothing and upholstered furniture are covered with the dog's hair. What is the best way to remove it?

Dip a clothes brush (used only for this purpose) in a bowl filled with water. Now brush the articles, removing hairs from the brush with a paper towel. With more toweling, blot dry the clothing or upholstered furniture and repeat the procedure until no hairs remain.

Why does a dog come in with his tail between his legs?

Because he has done something of which he is ashamed. He may have made a mess in the middle of your carpet, or he may have lost a fight with another dog.

Can you take your dog jogging with you?

Yes. But several precautions should be observed:

• Keep your dog on a leash.

• Do not run with him during the hottest part of the day, or in scorching summer weather, because he may suffer heat prostration.

• Do not let him run for long periods of time on blacktop or cinder paths, which can harm his paws.

• He should not run on the side near the road, and always run in the direction facing approaching traffic.

• Do not run with your dog if he does not appear to thoroughly enjoy this exercise.

• Check his paws when you return home.

The dog investigates everything he sees and hears. Is he too curious or is this normal behavior?

He is an alert, healthy dog and is acting just the way he should. This is how he will learn about people, places, objects, happenings, and other animals, so don't worry. A young, listless pup, merely sitting, paying little attention to what is going on around him, is the one who should concern you.

Feeding

- **How Much and When to Feed Your Pet**
- **Commercial Dog Food vs. Home-Cooked Meals**
- **Water, Water, Water**
- **Vitamins**
- **Minerals**
- **Overweight Dogs**
- **Finicky Eaters**
- **Treats**
- **Prescription Diets**
- **Diet Variety**

How much should your dog eat each day?

The quantity of food your dog should be fed varies according to his size, his age, the amount of exercise he receives, whether he is a working dog or a pet, and whether he lives outdoors or in the home. Your dog will be healthier if you feed him the proper amount of food required to keep him mentally and physically active, no more. The following is an approximate guide:

Weight of Dog (over one year old)	Food per Day Canned	Dry
7 – 14 pounds	1/2 pound	1 1/2 cups
15 – 29 pounds	1 pound	3 cups
30 – 40 pounds	2 pounds	4 1/2 cups
41 pounds and over	3 pounds	6 cups

• There are exceptions: Hunting and working dogs, and dogs that live in unheated outdoor kennels during the winter, should receive roughly 1/3 more food than noted in the chart. Pregnant and nursing dams need about two to three times more food than specified above and are fed two to four meals daily. Pups under one year old (but over two months), with a weight that corresponds to one in the chart, need about twice as much food as mentioned. Dogs under two months of age require about 1/8 pound of canned food or 1/3 cup of dry food.

What time should you feed your dog?

Age of Dog	8:00 A.M.	1:00 P.M.	3:00 P.M.	5:30 P.M.	10:30 P.M.
Weaning – 3 months old	X	X		X	X
3 – 6 months old	X		X		X
6 – 12 months old	X			X	
Over 12 months old	X————————OR————————X
		X————————TWO HALF-MEALS————————X

Your pet will need time to become accustomed to changes in his feeding schedule. The hour you choose to feed your pet does not have to conform exactly to the chart, but it should be as close as possible. In any case, give your dog fresh food at each meal, and feed him exactly at the same time(s) daily.

If the dog eats only one meal, when is the best time to serve it?

The most practical time for a pet to be fed is about 5:30 P.M., before you eat dinner. This prevents him from feeling left out or begging at the table. However, some people believe that different times of the morning, or even noon, are preferable. The most important point is to feed your dog regularly at the same time each day.

Should you feed your dog on home-cooked or commercially prepared food?

Commercial food is more sensible because preparing a home formula for your dog is very time consuming, and it is often more expensive. It rarely provides a balanced diet, and if your dog has to be boarded or hospitalized, he will be difficult to feed.

There are various types of commercially prepared dog food. How do they differ?

• *Dry:* This provides from 1200 to 1700 calories per pound and contains about 23% protein, 7.5% fat, 40% carbohydrates, and approximately 10% water. There are dry foods available that provide bulk to keep a dog from overeating, and there are some that require the addition of water, while others are ready-to-eat.

• *Canned:* This contains about 650 to 750 calories per pound and roughly 10% protein, 6% fat, 5% carbohydrates, and about 75% water.

• *Semi-moist:* This provides approximately 1200 calories per pound with about 20% protein, 6% fat, 35% carbohydrates, and 35% water.

Why does dog food contain so much water?

There is a great deal of water in dog food because meat contains about 70% water, and this is one of the staples of your dog's diet.

Does dry dog food only contain cereal?

Both dry and canned dog food contain meat, a necessity in every dog's diet. When you purchase dog food, buy known brands. Do not risk your pet's health with less expensive substitutes unless you are sure they are marketed by a reputable manufacturer.

How often does the dog need water?

Water should be available to your pet all the time so he can drink whenever he wants. Change the water at least once a day, although twice daily is better.

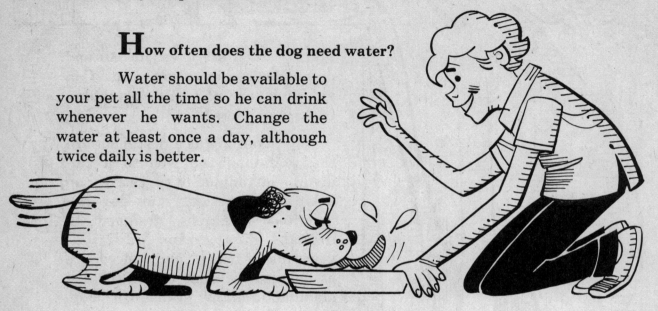

Should you add fat to your dog's food when his coat appears scruffy?

If you believe he needs more fat to improve his coat, add 1/4 to 1 1/2 teaspoons of corn oil daily to his food. Cooked egg yolks (not whites) will also improve his coat, and if it is not contained in the food you buy, add a yoke a day to his meal and you'll see a great improvement.

Is it all right to serve your dog raw steak?

You can feed your dog raw steak, but it must be supplemented with vitamins and minerals in order to provide a balanced diet.

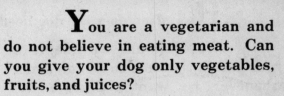

You are a vegetarian and do not believe in eating meat. Can you give your dog only vegetables, fruits, and juices?

Your dog is a descendant of the wolf, and the wolf is a carnivore—an animal who thrives on meat. As a result, your dog has inherited intestines designed to digest meat. In addition, vegetables, fruits, and juices are abundant in vitamin C, but the dog manufactures this in his own body. Meat, however, contains vital nutrients for his normal growth and development.

Is it better to serve baby food or puppy food to your pups?

Although you can use baby food, it is best to feed your pups food that has been especially formulated for them.

Will garlic keep your dog safe from worms?

Garlic will only make your dog's breath smell. There is no evidence that it has any effect on worms.

Your dog enjoys your cat's food, and the cat doesn't mind when the dog eats it. Should they continue to share the food?

No. Cat food is nutritionally deficient for dogs, and some have even become blind when cat food was primary in their diet. (The same happens when cats eat only dog food.) Feed your dog, dog food, your cat, cat food.

Why does the dog need vitamins?

Vitamin:	Aids:
A	Digestion, growth, eyesight, appetite
B	Circulation, skin maintenance, growth
C	Cellular tissue (Vitamin C is manufactured within the dog, and unless a veterinarian determines that your dog lacks it, it is unnecessary to add more to his diet.)
D	Bone development, teeth, growth
E	Circulation, fertility (Vitamin E is especially important for dams who are nursing young.)

Does your dog need minerals?

He does, and if you are not using commercially prepared food, which contains the correct ones in the right amount, you must add these to his meals: calcium, chlorine, copper, cobalt, iodine, iron, phosphorus, potassium, sodium, zinc.

What are prescription diets?

These are prepared foods available for every size, age, and type of dog. There are also special meal plans for dogs with kidney disfunctions, heart disease, other ailments, and for dogs who are obese, obtainable through a veterinarian.

When you eat breakfast, your dog wants to eat too. Should you feed him?

The aroma of your meal stimulates the dog's appetite. So give him a portion of his daily diet at breakfast and reserve the larger part for his main meal at night.

Should you vary your dog's diet?

Some dogs like variety in their diet, but most enjoy eating the same mixture day in and day out. In many cases, an alteration in diet will thoroughly upset a dog's stomach and bowels.

You were told not to serve your dog milk. Why?

Quite often, milk causes diarrhea in dogs. Omit it from your dog's diet if it loosens his bowels.

How do you choose the correct type of feeding dish?

Buy a durable dish that is easy to clean. A tiny dog needs a small, low dish. A long-nosed or long-eared pet requires a narrow, deep dish, and a large dog needs a heavy dish that won't slide or tip over when he eats.

Should your three adult dogs eat from the same dish?

Your dogs will probably be happier if they have their own dishes, and if they do, it will be easier to see that each consumes his necessary share of food. Always give the same dish to the same dog.

Your dog's ears trail in his food. What can you do?

When he eats, slip one leg of a pair of pantyhose over the top of your dog's head, tucking in his ears.

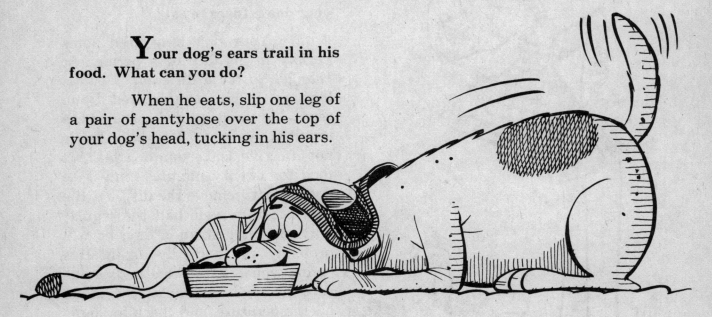

Is a raw knuckle bone good for your dog?

Your dog will derive great pleasure from gnawing on a raw knuckle bone, and it will stimulate his gastric juices, aiding in digestion. If your dog is teething, chewing on the bone will loosen his first set of milk teeth, accelerating the growth of the permanent ones. After he plays with the bone, rinse it with cool water. (If necessary, place it in the oven to make it crisp again, but don't give it to him when it's hot.) Check the bone frequently for splintering.

Does some dog food contain horse meat?

Yes. It is a wholesome source of protein. A high-grade horse meat is much more desirable than poor-grade beef scrap, and your dog won't experience any undesirable after-effects.

Are there some foods that are unsuitable for dogs?

Cabbage, brussels sprouts, cauliflower, turnips, potatoes, parsnips, salty items, pork (cooked or raw), and any food containing small bones or bones that splinter (fish, chicken, turkey, etc.) should not be fed to dogs.

Which high-protein food can you serve your dog?

Foods that are suitable for your dog and high in protein are meat, cooked egg yolks, and cheese (including cottage cheese).

What should you do when your dog refuses to eat?

Your dog may need some variety in his diet or a permanent change. So try a different meal, as long as it is manufactured by a reputable company and contains the required nutrients. If a new diet is not effective, leave your dog with his food for twenty minutes, and if he doesn't eat, remove the dish. At the next meal, provide half the regular portion. After about a day, he will probably eat normally again. But before you try this method, make sure the dog is not constipated, take his temperature, and check for signs of approaching or existing illness. Constipation and illness may be responsible for his lack of appetite.

Your dog is always hungry, but he is overweight. What should you do?

If you are certain that he does not have an illness that makes him appear overweight, cut down on his food immediately. An overweight or badly fed dog does not live as long as one with a trim figure and a balanced diet. Gradually decrease his intake, and eliminate food high in carbohydrates. If your dog becomes ravenous after his feeding, split his daily allowance in half and serve him twice, once in the morning and once at night.

Why do dogs eat grass?

Dogs eat grass instinctively; it cleans out their stomachs. However, if you use chemicals on your lawn or suspect that the grass he is eating has been chemically treated, pull your dog away from it. If necessary, give your dog some milk of magnesia—it will accomplish the same goal in a safer manner.

Your dog likes candy. Can you give him some occasionally?

Candy is high in calories and not very good for your dog's teeth, but a piece of candy every now and then shouldn't be too harmful.

Grooming

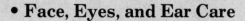

- **Face, Eyes, and Ear Care**
- **Cleaning Your Pet's Teeth**
- **Bathing a Small, Medium, or Large Dog**
- **Combing and Brushing**
- **Shedding**
- **Plucking and Clipping**
- **Matted Hair**
- **Treating Fleas, Ticks, and Lice**
- **Manicures**

Does a dog's face need to be washed every day?

Yes. He will find it very refreshing. Dip a facecloth in lukewarm water, wring it out, and wipe your dog's eyes, ears, and muzzle. Gently go over his front teeth and gums too.

Is it recommended to brush your dog's teeth?

Yes, but it is not an easy task. If you can dab his teeth with peroxide or tap water on a cotton swab, or spray his mouth with breath freshener, you will be accomplishing a great feat. However, if you cannot manage this and his breath becomes unbearable, take him to the vet for a professional cleaning.

Should a dog's teeth be checked periodically?

The teeth should not be troublesome after the initial teething period, provided the dog has been given plenty of things to chew and an occasional unsweetened, crunchy cookie. But when the dog eats only soft food, tartar will build up. The accumulation of too much tartar causes the gums to separate from the teeth, and the teeth will loosen or actually fall out. A vet should remove the tartar, but you can try to do it yourself, using a scraper made just for this purpose. It may be necessary to repeat the procedure every six months.

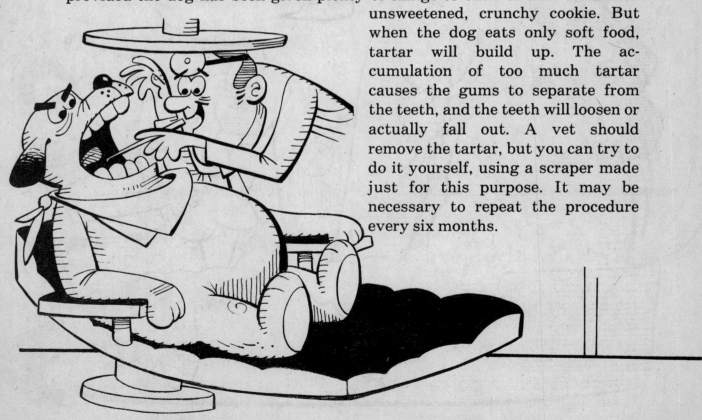

The dog's eyes run. What can you do?

Wipe away the discharge with cotton lightly soaked in boric acid solution. This rids the fur of stains. Generally, it is normal for dogs to have a slight discharge of the eyes. However, if the eyes seem inflamed, or the discharge looks more like pus, consult a vet immediately.

How do you take care of the dog's ears?

Examine his ears each week. To clear the canal of wax and dirt, gently wipe the interior with mineral oil on a cotton swab. Do not probe too deeply and hold your dog's head firmly so he cannot make a quick move, resulting in an unintended jab. Look for mites, ticks, and other parasites—this is one of their favorite hiding spots. A nasty odor or actual discharge from the ears should be brought to the attention of the veterinarian.

Should you plug the dog's ears and oil his eyes before his bath?

The dog may not react well to seeing and hearing improperly. Try not to get soap in his eyes or water in his ears. But if you are afraid that you might, spread a drop or two of mineral oil along the dog's eyelids, and put a couple of drops in each eye. Plug each ear with a long, thin swab of absorbent cotton. Before inserting, dab the ends with petroleum jelly and place the jelly-covered tips in the dog's ears. The ointment acts as a water repellent and helps keep the plugs in place.

How often do dogs need a bath? Do they like baths?

Your dog should be bathed about every three months—frequently enough to keep him clean without destroying his natural oils. (Dogs younger

than six months should not be bathed yet.) Use a mild shampoo for normal hair, not a dog shampoo that treats lice, ticks, and other parasites, unless your pet is actually troubled by them, because the mixture is too harsh for his skin. Some dogs enjoy the soothing effects of soaping and scalp massaging while others work themselves into a frenzy. Have another person stand by during your dog's first bath in case you need help—your dog's behavior is unpredictable.

What is the procedure for bathing a medium-size dog?

You will need a deep, unbreakable tub suitable for the size of your dog; a sponge; shampoo; and many, many towels. Make sure the dog has relieved himself before you begin.

Place the dog in the empty tub. Once he is settled, *slowly* pour warm water (approximately 75°F.) from a jug until the water level reaches his hocks—he will either be fascinated by the rising water or distressed, struggling to free himself. Therefore, all windows, doors, and other possible routes of escape should be blocked, especially if you remove his collar.

Now, trickle water on one part of his body, apply shampoo, and wash and massage this area. Proceed, section by section. To clean his face, wring out the sponge in *plain warm water,* wipe the eye area and dry the entire face immediately. Do not let suds drip into his eyes. And don't forget to wash inside the ears and under the flaps, and again, dry quickly and thoroughly. Shampoo his genitals and under his tail quickly, rinsing the soap before it stings him. While bathing your dog, speak softly to him, telling him how beautiful he will look—you want the bath to be a pleasant experience for both of you.

When the bathing is completed, either lift your dog from the tub or ask him to step out. Empty the soapy water, return the dog to the tub, and *slowly* refill the tub with warm water. Rinse him, repeating as often as necessary.

Finally, empty the tub once more and return the dog to it. Use two hands to press out surplus water, then rub him vigorously with a towel. Do this as quickly as possible so the dog does not have a chance to shake himself, showering you and everything else nearby.

Take the dog out of the tub and continue rubbing, pausing occasionally to allow him to shake himself now. Dry his paws well. When he is fairly dry, snuggle him into another towel and keep rubbing. Then brush and comb his fur (if he wants to lie down, place a towel underneath him).

After the bath, place the dog in a warm room (about 72°F.), and check on him every fifteen minutes. Do not permit him outdoors, under any circumstances, for three or four hours. With one more brushing and combing, he will look like a dog again.

How do you bathe a 125-pound dog?

It will have to be done in the bathtub, and ideally, he should step into and out of the tub himself. It will be difficult to get him in, and you will have a harder time getting him out. Therefore, the very best way to bathe a 125-pound dog is to let a groomer, knowledgeable in handling large canines, do it.

Is there any way to prevent your dog from slipping in the bath?

Use rubber mats, one in the bottom of the tub and another at the point where he steps out. Make sure each mat is large enough to meet the needs of his size. All four paws should rest squarely on the mat; otherwise, the chances of him slipping are increased.

Does a dog need a bath after he swims in the ocean?

The salt water will spoil his coat, and unfortunately, sewage is drained into many oceans. So, give your dog a bath after his swim, and don't allow dogs younger than six months old into the ocean.

Are there dogs who should never be bathed?

Some people do not believe in bathing dogs at all. Most of the Spitz breeds do not require baths, but their owners sometimes clean them, using a spirit or dry shampoo. These same methods can be employed on any other breeds. Dry shampoos are also good to use on young or ill dogs and on a female who is close to giving birth.

You gave your dog a bath, groomed him, let him out, and he came home smothered in dirt. Why did he do this?

Dogs like to smell and look like dogs. They will follow their inborn habit of camouflaging themselves to remain undetected, and it is doubtful that you can break this pattern of behavior. Therefore, you will have to keep on his tail to make sure it and he stay clean.

In rainy weather your dog returns home with a distinctive, unpleasant odor. Is this natural?

If your dog has had a bath every three months and licks himself clean in between, he should not smell bad. Keep an old towel near the door and give him a vigorous rub when he comes indoors. Make sure his paws are completely dry.

The dog wreaks from a horrible odor, not the natural "doggy smell." What is it?

This stench comes from the dog's anus because the glands need evacuating. You can empty the dog's glands yourself. Cover your table with

plenty of newspaper and place your dog on it. Have paper towels ready, and with the left hand, lift the dog's tail to reveal the anus. Two glands are situated on either side. Using the right hand, take your thumb and index finger and apply firm pressure, squeezing the glands upward and together. When the contents start expelling, quickly grasp the paper towels and wipe clean. Repeat until the discharge ceases and the glands are empty. Then wash the anal area with warm water. Your dog may need this attention at regular intervals, so examine him once a month.

Is it true that you can improve the color of your dog's coat with rinses and dyes?

Yes. There are rinses available to make apricot dogs more orange, black dyes to enrich the color of your black-coated pets, blues to make your grey dogs greyer, and blues to make your white dogs purer. Special chalk is used to improve the tones of wirehairs. None of these treatments will harm your animal's coat, although they will exempt him from competing in official shows.

How can you groom your dog at home?

Grooming should never be considered a chore, because your dog will sense your dislike and won't enjoy it either. Grooming keeps his coat clean and healthy, and his skin supple and in good condition. Use the appropriate animal brush and comb for your type of dog. Tend to your pet at least three times a week.

• *Short smooth-haired breeds:* First, with a short-bristled brush (not nylon), rid the dog's coat of dandruff and dust. Brush all areas, including underbody, limbs, and paws. Then go over him with a hound glove (available in most pet shops), and to add a sleek and glossy finish, run a nylon cloth over his entire body. Your dog will be neat and clean in ten minutes, from start to finish.

• **Densely-coated breeds:** Twenty-minute sessions result in a well-groomed dog. Use a coarse-toothed comb and a brush with bristles (not nylon) that are long enough to reach through the fur to his skin. Lift the hair in sections, from his tail up to his head, brushing and combing upward. Now brush it down again unless a stand-off coat is in style for your breed.

• **Wirehaired breeds:** You will need a stiff brush with bristles (not nylon) set at an angle and, again, long enough to penetrate through the dog's fur to his skin. Comb to loosen all tangles and remove dead hair, and then brush thoroughly. Check for hairs growing in his ears and cut or pluck them weekly. He should have a complete stripping, plucking, and trimming three times a year. This is best done by a professional groomer, but you can do it yourself. Instructional books are available for specific breeds.

The Terrier's coat needs to be plucked. How do you do it?

It is strongly advised that you take your dog to a groomer for this, because when done wrong, you can hurt the dog or make his skin very sore afterward. Uneven work will look moth-eaten, and your fingers will ache because the task takes a long time to complete. However, if you insist, this is the way: Start at the base of the neck and work downward, leaving the head and face until last. Pick up a small section of the dog's coat, and when you find *dead* hair, tweak it out by pulling with the thumb and index finger in a downward twist. Do not break off the hair. Repeat for the entire coat. *Plucking must never be attempted until the dog is already in the stage of molting*—it is intended to encourage growth of the new, upcoming coat.

61

Do dogs shed all the time or does it just seem that way?

Dogs generally shed their coats once or twice a year—in late spring and fall. In addition, bitches lose their coats after delivering a litter. Temperature also affects shedding: it will occur more often during scorching spells or in a very hot home. It takes approximately six weeks for the new coat to replace the old. This happens so gradually that there should never be any bare patches. If there are, then the dog is ill. During the shedding period, be meticulous. Brushing and combing the dog to loosen dead hairs will encourage the growth of new ones.

Can you learn to clip your poodle?

It's great fun to create the Lion Trim and other fashionable styles, and in no time, you will become an expert. (Purchase an instructional manual to learn all the cuts.) If you make a mistake, don't worry. It will grow back quickly. Just shorten the hair all over, and you will have the Puppy Clip.

How do you rid your dog of matted hair?

Saturate the mat with almond oil. With your fingers, a stiff brush, and the end tooth of a comb, work on it gently to untangle the hairs. Grip the fur close to the roots to prevent pulling the dog's skin and hurting him. In many cases, the mat will simply have to be cut off. Try to perform this task in the most artistic fashion possible. In any event, never give the dog a bath before combing through the matting. Wet hair is completely unmanageable.

Is there a way to prevent fur from matting?

Prevention is certainly preferable to cure. Freq... best preventative. Special attention should be given to... the ears, beneath the tail, the haunches, between the toes,... pads. If your pet is not going to compete in shows, lea... tractively in the spots where matting most often occurs. Ma... uncomfortable, and unhealthy, so tend to it regularly.

Does the texture of a dog's coat change as he grows old...

Yes. Many pups have soft fluffy fur, but as they age, it g... s coarse. The change becomes apparent at about four months old. (The dog acquires his full adult coat usually by the time he is about one year old.)

Can a flea collar be harmful?

A flea collar is fine for preventing fleas, and no four-paws should be without one. However, replace it every three months; otherwise it loses its effectiveness. Tighten it every two weeks because it tends to stretch. *Never allow the collar to get wet.* Moisture releases its chemical content and this frequently causes skin inflammation. If the dog has been out in the rain, remove the collar immediately. Don't forget to take it off before the dog goes for a swim. Some canines are allergic to flea collars, so if your dog protests strongly after wearing it for two or three days, stop using it.

Where do ticks usually hide?

They hide anywhere there is perspiration or soft skin and warmth— around the dog's ears, between the pads of his paws, between his toes, under his tail, near the sex organs. Check his coat, sifting through the fur to observe the skin. Also examine his bedding, chair, and all his favorite spots. Scratching is a sure sign of ticks.

...cks harm dogs?

...heir bites can become
...ed, and they usually cause skin
...uptions from the dog's ceaseless
scratching. When totally unchecked,
they produce jaundice and paralysis.
And they may drain so much blood
from the animal that he becomes
anemic and apathetic. Ticks can
send your dog to an early grave.

How do you relieve your dog of ticks?

You will need a pair of tweezers and a bowl filled with vinegar. With
your fingers, separate the dog's fur until you see his skin. When you spot a
tick, grasp it securely in the tweezers and pull in a *straight* upward motion. Do
not pull slantwise because the tick's body may break with the head still
embedded in the dog. Drop the tick in the vinegar, wipe the tweezers with a
paper towel, and repeat. After you are finished, burn the ticks. Do not flush
them down the sink or toilet; they can survive in water. And be careful: people
can become infected by picking ticks from their dogs. You must use tweezers
and, if possible, wear gloves.

How do you get rid of lice?

If your dog is so seriously infested that commercial flea powder is not effective, see a groomer. He will treat him with the proper solution. It is difficult to do yourself, and the longer you put it off, the worse the problem becomes. Throw away all of the dog's bedding, either by placing it in plastic bags or, preferably, by burning it. Smaller items may be sprayed with a suitable insecticide and/or washed in hot, soapy water. Regular grooming is the way to catch sight of parasites such as ticks, but lice are so minute that only through the dog's consistent scratching are you likely to be aware of their presence. Your house may be infested too. Summon an insect exterminator: these pests multiply so rapidly, you must use every means to rid your dog and your home of them.

Is the dog supposed to have a manicure? His claws are very long.

Dogs that get a good deal of exercise on stone sidewalks usually wear down their claws. However, those who lead a more immobile existence or trot about on soft ground do need their nails shortened every two to four weeks. You can buy a pair of nail clippers for dogs and do it yourself. Do not clip the nails too low, cutting them to the quick. Use an emery board to smooth the edges of each nail. Don't forget to trim and file the dewclaws. They are found above the paws on the inside of the hind legs. Most people have these surgically removed, but for showing purposes, it is required that they are left intact for the Briard and Great Pyrenees breeds.

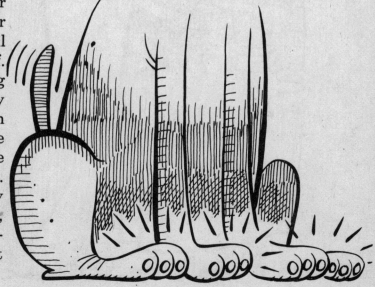

Training

The pet store owner insisted that you buy a choke collar to train your dog. Isn't there a kinder method?

The choke collar will not choke your dog; it simply tightens around his neck, letting him know when you don't like what he is doing and encouraging him to stop. Purchase a *good* metal choke collar, smoothly electroplated with small, close metal links—large, open links tend to entangle and hurt the dog. The dog sports his choke collar during training and wears his fine leather collar at all other times.

Why can't you use a regular collar for training?

If a dog is wearing a regular leather or nylon collar and you use the corrective jerk, the collar might jar his windpipe, creating permanent damage. Also, dogs usually learn to slip out of their regular collars before learning anything else. A choke collar, attached to the leash you are holding, is insurance against your pet's escape.

Are there any other items you will need to train your dog?

It is a waste of money to buy a great deal of complex equipment. A choke collar, a leather leash (standard size is 6 feet long), and a noisemaker are all you need, and you can make the noisemaker yourself: Fill an empty beer or soda can with about one dozen pebbles or pennies and securely seal the opening. Then, cover the entire can with a piece of cloth tied at both ends.

Why is it difficult for some people to train their dogs while others have no trouble at all?

A dog can be trained to do many things, but most people are not patient and consistent. They scold the animal for something they do not like one time, then encourage the very same act later. First concentrate on paper training your dog. After he has mastered this, give him lessons in other acts.

Should you use a loud, booming voice when instructing your dog?

No. Training should be fun. Employ loving caresses to prompt the correct behavior, the dog earning and enjoying your affectionate responses. Speak firmly and issue commands in a well-modulated tone. Shrillness and shouting will upset the dog because his hearing is very keen, and anger accomplishes nothing, except, perhaps, the ill-will of your dog.

You beat the dog, but he still does the wrong things. What can you do?

A dog must be consistently disciplined, but not beaten. Like most canines, he probably wants to gain your approval, but unless you have the patience to train him properly, he will not know what pleases you and what makes you angry. If the dog, however, is a constant source of irritation, it might be best to find a good home for him elsewhere, before you seriously injure him or he fights back and harms you.

How long should each obedience session last?

For a dog under 15 pounds, sessions should be held for five minutes, twice a day, with at least four hours between lessons. For a dog from 16 to 45 pounds, ten minutes, twice a day, with the same intermission period. For an animal weighing over 45 pounds, fifteen minutes, twice a day, and again, with four hours between sessions. Concentrate on one new act at a time, with a quick review of previously learned exercises. Do not proceed to a new discipline until the dog has become fairly accomplished at the last one.

TODAY'S LESSON...
...10 MINUTES!
FETCH!

Is it difficult to teach a dog elementary commands?

The shorter the command, the quicker the dog will understand. Always use the same words, in the same sequence, and in the same tone of voice to convey the same meaning. Pretend you are angry when the dog does something you do not like, but don't lose control. Always use the dog's name first when instructing and praising him. Do not use his name when he disobeys and you are "angry." If he fails to understand your displeasure, reinforce your words, "B-a-d, b-a-d," with a rattle or a noisemaker. Never use your hand to hit him, for he will react to it as if it is a weapon in the future, and never lash your dog with a whip or chain.

What is the first command to teach Pete, your dog?

Train him to "Sit" on your *left*. While holding the leash in your *right* hand, use your *left* hand to push the dog's hindquarters firmly, and pleasantly say, "Pete, Sit." Do this until he actually sits, and keep him in this position for a few minutes by maintaining pressure. Check his posture: He should be sitting upright with his front legs slanting outward very slightly, his head, nicely poised, his eyes looking straight at you. If he slumps to one side or rests on one hip, ease him into the required, more elegant position, then praise him lavishly. When he responds without prodding, remove his training collar and leash and merely give the verbal command.

The dog has learned to "Sit," but he gets up immediately. What can you do?

If he responds to your command "Sit," then a few seconds later, after having met his obligation, gets up and runs around, you must teach him the "Sit-Stay" command. (This command is intended for home use only.) Do not force him to remain in one position for a very long period because it is unkind, and do not make him "Stay" when you are doing something he might want to join. Perhaps, for instance, the family is sitting around a cozy fire roasting chestnuts. Don't make the dog sit on the fringes of the room where it is cold and he will feel left out. If you don't want him in the room, put him someplace where he cannot see what you are doing.

How do you teach your dog the "Sit-Stay" command?

To teach your dog to "Sit-Stay," he must be wearing his leash and choke collar. First command him to "Sit" on your *left*. When your dog is seated, block his vision: Place the fingers of your *left* hand together. (Your *right* hand is holding the leash.) Then lean down in front of the dog, and with your left hand, block the dog's vision about 3 inches away from his eyes, moving your hand from side to side once. Now, without using the dog's name, say, "Stay," and return your hand to your side. When the dog understands what is expected, he will respond to the hand signal without the vocal command, or vice versa. This is *Stage I.*

You taught the dog to "Sit" and "Sit-Stay," and he performs perfectly. But when you move, he moves too. What can you do?

There are extensions of the "Sit-Stay" command and they must be mastered by you and your dog in step-by-step fashion.

• *Stage II:* Your goal now is to reverse your position while the dog remains sitting. Execute this in the following manner: Your dog is in "Sit-Stay" on your *left.* You are both looking straight ahead. In as few moves as possible, start with your *right* foot and reverse your body, bringing it directly in front of your dog. (*Never begin your action with your left foot* because the dog will misinterpret it as a "Heel" signal.) In your new position, your feet should be placed together. While reversing your position, pull the dog's leash up and *behind* (so you do not hit his nose) his head. This will require 18 to 30 inches of leash (according to the size of your dog) held taut while the rest of the 6-foot leash remains loosely in your *right* hand with your thumb through the loop. Do not pull the leash so that it chokes the dog, but don't leave it too slack. He must be aware of it. The object is to merely lift his neck and collar *slightly* so he cannot move when you do. With practice, you will become accomplished at reversing your position and tightening the leash simultaneously, and he will learn to respond properly. Request that he remain in position for thirty seconds after your transition, then praise him profusely. Next, command him to "Relax." A few minutes later, repeat the procedure.

• *Stage III* begins at the point where you are facing the dog, holding the leash above his head in your *right* hand. Transfer the leash to your *left* hand and place your thumb inside the loop. With your *right* hand, palm up, place four fingers under the leash and your thumb on top of the leash, about 18 inches from the dog's collar. Hold this length taut by using thumb pressure. The remainder of the leash is held slack in your *left* hand. Now, back away from the dog, sliding your *right* hand up the leash as you move. This means a longer length of leash will remain taut. If the dog rises to follow, repeat the command "Stay," and step toward him in the starting position—leash held taut above his head. When the dog reseats himself, praise him. Then after a brief pause, begin Stage III again. Each time you repeat the procedure you will probably be able to move farther and farther away before the dog attempts to follow. The goal in Stage III is to move 6 feet from the dog—the length of the leash—while he remains seated. Do not attempt to accomplish this in one session. It will take several periods of practice, so be patient.

• In *Stage IV,* the dog remains in "Sit-Stay" while you walk to the left and to the right. Place your dog in "Sit-Stay," and proceed to the point in Stage II where you are facing the dog, holding the leash in your *right* hand taut above his head. Now, start with your *right* foot and take two steps to the *left,* keeping the leash taut. Return. Then, start with your *right* foot and step to the *right.* These movements may be awkward for you, but this is only an exercise and will soon be discontinued. The dog is permitted a minor amount of head-turning during Stage IV, but make sure he does not raise his hindquarters off the floor or reseat himself in order to watch you.

• In *Stage V,* the dog remains in "Sit-Stay" while you circle him. Start with "Sit-Stay," and continue through Stage II to the point where you are facing the dog, holding the leash taut above his head in your *right* hand. Beginning with your *right* foot, walk in a complete circle around your dog. If he attempts to follow, pull the leash tighter and repeat the command "Stay." Take fairly large steps; do not tip-toe or shuffle. It will take some time for the dog to learn to stay in place while you circle him, but when he remains in position for a reasonable period, praise him. Also praise him before you end each session.

What is "heeling"? How can you teach Pete to heel?

Heeling is a discipline that prevents your dog from pulling you, stopping to sniff rubbish, visiting trees, and following squirrel trails. It means he walks when you walk and stops when you stop. Have the animal walk on your *left*, his nose in line with your thigh, and execute heeling in the following manner: Hold the leash in your *right* hand (with your right hand loose at your side), allowing the dog about 3 feet of leash. Order your dog to "Sit." Then say, "Pete, Heel," and start walking, taking your first step with your *left* foot. Pete will rise and move with you. If he tries pulling ahead, let him do this until the full 6 feet of the leash has been extended, then abruptly reverse direction, shorten the leash to 3 feet, repeat "Pete, Heel," and continue walking the opposite way. Pete will at first be startled by your abrupt command, the tightening of the leash, and the sudden turn, but he will be forced to accompany you. If Pete keeps pace, praise him and keep going. If he leaps ahead of you, repeat the procedure.

Your animal becomes tired of remaining in the "Sit" position. Is there a better position suitable for long periods of time?

If you wish your dog to remain in one spot for a long period, use the "Down" and "Down-Stay" commands.

• *Stage I* ("Down"): Place your dog in "Sit-Stay" on your *left*. Kneel on your *left* knee, lean over and grasp his two front paws in your hand by placing your thumb on the outside of his *right* paw, index finger between his two paws, and your other three fingers on the outside of his *left* paw. Then, gently pull him forward so he has no option but to lower himself. As you are easing him forward, command him to "D---O---W---N" so that the word takes as long to say as the animal takes to reach the floor. When he completes this, be sure to praise him. Each time he fails, place him in "Sit-Stay" and begin again. He may roll over on one side or become playful once he's on the floor. If he does this, don't mete out any punishment, but after permitting a few seconds of frivolity, command him to the "Sit-Stay" position and repeat the exercise.

• *Stage II* ("Down-Stay"): "Down-Stay" is easily mastered if the dog obeys the "Down" and "Sit-Stay" commands. With the dog in the "Down" position, walk around him or away from him. If he begins to get up, say "Stay." When he returns to position, praise him.

Should you use a command—for instance, "Heel" or "Sit"—to stop mischievous behavior?

Do not confuse commands with corrections. Let's say the dog has your tablecloth in his mouth. If you command him to "Sit," he might sit with the cloth still clenched in his teeth, bringing down all your fine china on his head. He cannot understand that you want him to finish one act before he begins another. So, use "No!" or "B-a-d" when correcting your dog. After he obeys, command him to "Sit" or "Heel."

A dog should not be punished, he should be corrected. If you don't like repeating the word "B-a-d," then use "No!" In any event, your tone of voice must be firm and masterful and the same word must be used consistently. Avoid interchanging words or speaking them in unison—for instance, "No, Oliver, you are bad. Naughty. Shame on you. Bad. No." Remember, *never add the dog's name when reprimanding him.* If the dog obeys the verbal command, no further action is necessary. If he doesn't obey, repeat the corrective words "B-a-d, b-a-d" or "No! No!" and then shake the noisemaker. Do not speak and shake the noisemaker at the same time. (Eventually, you want the dog to respond to either stimulus alone.)

Always stare directly into your dog's eyes when you are giving orders. True or False?

Sometimes a dog is impossible to control. The direct stare, combined with verbal commands and hand signals, is a most effective way to let your dog know who is in charge. Nevertheless, it is nicer to foster a loving relationship in which the dog behaves because he adores you.

What tricks can your dog learn?

Do not *expect* your dog to be a trickster. Some canines have a natural aptitude, while others are more capable of performing other deeds. So, if your dog does not take to learning certain tricks, forget about them. However, there are dogs who can shake hands, play dead, roll over, bring the newspaper, fetch slippers, retrieve and throw a ball, dive in water to retrieve objects, dribble a ball, catch tidbits, climb a stepladder, call someone to dinner, play hide-and-seek, and walk on their hind legs.

How can you train your German Shepherd to become a guard dog?

Do not train your dog to be vicious. You may unleash great hostility, which later may be directed at you, at an innocent child, or at a friend. Rather, take your pet to an experienced, reputable, professional trainer, someone who specializes in guard-dog training.

Should you send your dog to an obedience training school if you don't want to train him yourself?

It is a great idea and well worth the price, but find a reliable trainer to carry out the task. Several different methods are available: You and the dog attend school together, learning at the same time; the dog is sent away to be trained, then you are instructed on handling him, learning the responses to expect to specific commands; a trainer comes into your home, teaching both of you there.

What basic words and commands should you use to train your dog?

Say:	To:
"Heel" or "To Heel"	Make him come to heel or walk to heel
"Stay"	Order him to remain in position
"Sit"	Request that he sit
"Down"	Make him lie down
"Hush"	Silence him
"Good Dog"	Show approval

"Bad Dog"	Show disapproval
"Hurry"	Speed up his actions
"Sleeping Time"	Tell him it is time to go to bed

"No"	Stop him from doing something
"Drop It"	Make him release something
"Fetch"	Request him to retrieve
"Relax"	Communicate rest time

You can compose your own commands, but make sure different commands do not sound alike. For instance, do not say "Bed" to signify bedtime. It might sound like "Bad" to the dog. And use the same words, in the same sequence, each time you wish to convey the same meaning.

How do you teach your dog to shake hands?

Command your dog to "Sit." Then take his right paw and shake it while saying "How do you do?" or "Hello, how are you?" After a while, your dog may raise his paw without your assistance whenever you say these words. If you command him to do this anytime a visitor enters the house, he may also go into his act to greet all newcomers.

Can you teach your pet to fetch a newspaper?

Yes. If you have the newspaper delivered, it may either be rolled, or it may be delivered flat. If it is rolled, pick up the newspaper and place it between your dog's teeth. Then lead your dog to your favorite chair. If the newspaper is flat, teach him to drag it by putting his teeth firmly around the fold of the newspaper. In no time at all, you may be able to remain seated and command your dog to "Fetch the newspaper," and he will do so.

Can a dog be taught to climb a ladder?

Put your dog's front paws on the second rung of a ladder and his back paws on the first rung. Then have a second person *gently* push your pet's back paws onto the second rung while you raise his front paws to the third rung, and say "Climb the ladder." If the dog seems frightened or completely unable to do this, do not proceed with this trick.

Can you command the dog to dive in water to recover an object?

Throw an object into the water, then command the dog to fetch it, saying "Fetch." Do not encourage your dog to go into very cold water to perform this trick, or to jump in and out of water under a hot sun. Rather, teach your dog the trick in warm, mild weather, and do not repeat the command more than six times.

How do you teach your dog to play dead?

Command your dog to lie down. Then turn him on his right side, put the palms of your hands on his body, and press down lightly but firmly. Remove your hands and say "Play dead." After a time, he may lie down and remain motionless when you merely utter the words "Play dead."

Can your dog learn to dribble a ball?

This is a little more difficult for your dog to learn, but it's worth a try. Give your dog a ball and push his nose near it. Move his head *very* gently so that his nose comes in contact with the ball, giving it a little push. Repeat again and again and see if he catches onto the idea. You can use the accompanying phrase "Dribble ball."

What is the best way to instruct your dog to "Say prayers"?

Command your dog to sit, facing the bed. Place his paws on the side of the bed at a level slightly lower than his nose. Next, *gently* push his head down so that his nose is between his paws and say "Say prayers."

Is it easy for your pet to roll over?

This trick has to be taught in two steps.

• *Step 1:* Command you dog to lie on the floor and turn him on his right side. Bend his front paws in toward his body, then *gently* roll him over. Say "Roll over."

• *Step 2:* When your dog has accomplished this, tell him to "Roll over," and when he has done so, show him how to roll over again. Keep him away from furniture into which he might crash in his enthusiasm to keep on rolling.

How do you teach your pet to catch tidbits?

Throw a biscuit, or any tidbit, in the direction of his nose. Say "Catch." If he responds, repeat, throwing the biscuit a little higher each time until he reaches his limit.

Can you teach your dog to do something useful or different?

Of course you can, and here are some suggestions:

• *Fetch handbag or briefcase:* Show the dog the handbag or briefcase, allowing him to sniff at it if he wishes. Then take him some distance away from the object and issue the command—perhaps "Handbag." Note your body movements as you speak and always say the same word(s) accompanied by the same body movements for the same effect. Your consistency will improve your chances of getting your dog to learn quickly. When he catches on to what you want him to do, you will no longer have to show him the handbag. Simply issue the verbal command.

• *Watch TV:* The aim is to make your dog sit in front of the television set as if he wishes to watch his favorite program. Use the command "Sit," but make sure your dog is facing the TV set when you say this, and instead of just saying "Sit," say "Sit, watch TV."

• *Bury the trash:* This trick comes in handy if family members are in the habit of leaving soda cans, or other items to be disposed of, around the house. Take the dog outside, show him the soda can, then take his front paws and make digging motions with them. If he continues to dig, when the hole becomes big enough, drop in the can and, using his paws, show him how to cover it up again. The dog should *already* be accustomed to burying bones and other items without instruction from anyone to master this trick easily.

• *Retrieve golf balls:* This is a practical trick if you are a golfer, or you might even persuade a golf range to hire your dog to retrieve balls for a small fee. Place your dog's nose near a golf ball and encourage him to pick it up. When he has mastered this, show him a bucket, then open his mouth *gently* so the ball drops into the bucket. After a while, your dog may perform both these feats by himself whenever he sees golf balls, but keep him off the course when people are playing; otherwise, the golfers may not be too enthusiastic about your dog's new trick.

• *Sing:* Play one special song and howl along. Soon, you may find your dog imitating you.

Some dogs will be good subjects for training, while others will just not be able to learn, no matter what you do. Always praise your pet lavishly when he tries to do what you want, but *never, never* punish him if he finds it impossible to be a trickster.

How do you teach your pet to fetch someone for dinner?

When dinner is on the table, wave your arm in the direction of the person you want fetched and say "Fetch Jane, dinner is ready." Always use the same tone of voice and the same body movements. Take the dog to Jane if he doesn't seem to understand, then bring Jane back with the two of you and seat her at the table. Note: Do not say the word "dinner" if you use it with the dog when referring to *his* meal.

How does a dog learn to fetch slippers?

Place the slippers some distance away, then sit in your favorite chair and wave your arm in the direction of the slippers. If the dog does not seem to understand, walk him to the slippers, place one in his mouth, say "Fetch slippers," and accompany him back to the chair. Remove the slipper from his mouth and set it down next to you. Then go back with the dog to the next slipper and repeat.

You saw a Poodle retrieve and throw a ball on his hind legs. Will it be difficult for your Poodle to learn this trick?

Poodles are great at this trick because they have a natural tendency to walk on their hind legs. Place a ball some distance away, then say "Fetch ball on hind legs," taking hold of the dog's front paws and walking him on his hind legs to the ball. Put the ball in his mouth and walk him back. After he has accomplished this and when he has the ball in his mouth, tell him to "Throw ball." Show him how this should be done by *gently* removing the ball from his mouth, *gently* bouncing it off his nose, then throwing it upward and slightly forward above his nose.

Is it true that a dog can be taught to read?

Yes. But it will take a great deal of patience and consistency.

• *Step 1:* Write on an oblong piece of cardboard the word "S H O E." Then command the dog to fetch a shoe—perhaps pointing in the proper direction—which you have previously placed a short distance away. Next, show the dog the cardboard with the word "S H O E" on it and verbally command him to fetch a shoe. Repeat this several times.

• *Step 2:* Show the dog the cardboard, do not say anything, but use the same body movements—pointing—as when you gave him the verbal command to fetch the shoe.

When he has mastered this, try a new word printed on a triangular piece of cardboard. For instance, if you want him to jump up into his chair, write the word "J U M P" or "C H A I R" and repeat Steps 1 and 2.

Practice this trick with your dog for a total of five or ten minutes each day, and allow him to take as long as necessary to master one word before going on to the next. The secret lies in using a different shaped or sized piece of cardboard for each new instruction and employing exactly the same body movements when you silently show him the cardboard as when you verbally issue the command.

If your dog responds to the first two steps, you can add words to build up his vocabulary. Here are some other words you might try:

Written Command	Cardboard Shape	Action Required
D I N N E R	Oval	Fetch someone for dinner
H A M M E R	Square	Go to the garage and fetch a hammer (if the dog is big enough for this)
N E W S P A P E R	Circle	Fetch a newspaper

For a finishing touch to your act, use different-colored cards. Even though your dog cannot detect colors, he will see them in various shades of grey.

Can a dog be trained to catch a Frisbee?

Most dogs have a natural instinct to chase after any moving object. But if your dog is simply not interested or pants far too much when engaged in a chase, he is obviously not a candidate for a good game of catch, and should not be forced to take part.

A dog weighing over 35 pounds is best suited to play the game, but strong small dogs might also be physically able to participate. Before you introduce your pet to the game, it is wise to have your veterinarian check your animal to make sure that he is in the proper physical condition to run and strenuously leap into the air. Some breeds are predisposed to hip, joint, or spinal problems, and it is particularly important that they receive regular check-ups if they partake in Frisbee-catching.

When you and your dog are playing with the Frisbee, you *MUST* have water available nearby so your dog can drink as much as he wants anytime he wants.

What is the best surface for Frisbee playing?

The ground should be soft, with grass the best of all. Hard asphalt, concrete, and dry sand are definitely not suitable because the dog's legs will slip, possibly resulting in injury. Sea-wet sand is better, but continued practice upon it may cause your pet to contract rheumatism.

How do you train your dog to catch a Frisbee?

• *Step 1:* Roll the Frisbee along the ground and command your dog to "Fetch." The dog should run after the disc and return it to you. Repeat this for five minutes on the first day, increasing the practice time by one minute each day until you reach a maximum of ten minutes per session. Then you are ready for Step 2.

• *Step 2:* Stoop down and throw the Frisbee at the dog's eye level. Command him to "Fetch." Again, do this for five minutes the first day, increasing the practice time by one minute each day until the dog is busily engaged in catching and fetching for a period of ten minutes.

• *Step 3:* Hold the Frisbee about 6 inches over the dog's head and command the dog to "Jump" to obtain it. Increase the height by 1 inch each day if the dog does not experience any great difficulty in jumping. Do not force the dog to jump higher if he simply can't manage to do so. This exercise should be carried out for five minutes each day for a total of six days. Do not exceed this limit because your dog's muscles must be strengthened *gradually.* Allow your dog to rest on the seventh day, then proceed to Step 4.

• *Step 4:* Throw the Frisbee a short distance into space, let your dog chase after it, and, if he can, catch it. Again, practice this for five minutes during the first session and increase the time by one minute daily until you reach a maximum of ten minutes. On the seventh day, let your pet rest. Try to throw the Frisbee evenly so that the dog can successfully catch it often. Be sure to praise him profusely after every attempt, whether he succeeds in his endeavor or not. And never scold him; this must always be a game—not torture!

• *Step 5:* Now is the time for creative throwing. You can toss the disc at great speed or very slowly. Spin it. Whatever you do, take note of the height and angle of the throw that is best for your dog, keeping failure to a minimum. Each session should last twenty minutes.

When you resume practice, throw the Frisbee farther and farther away and command your dog to chase and fetch.

The Growing Dog

The neighbors complain that your dog barks incessantly when you are away from home. What can you do?

Before you leave the house, put his collar and leash on, and when he barks, use a corrective jerk and say "B-a-d" in a firm tone. Then walk out of the house and listen. If he begins to bark, dash back inside and deliver the corrective jerk and say "B-a-d" in an angry tone, but praise him after he quiets down.

Your dog constantly barks because he is lonely and bored. If he is alone most of the time, the kindest action you can take is to find a new home for him where he will have more companionship.

When the doorbell rings, the dog barks. How do you quiet him?

Distract his attention. Drop something close behind that will make a noise as it hits the floor. (A magazine should work.) When he turns around, give the "Hush" command.

The dog scratches the door when he wants to enter the house. How can you prevent him from ruining the door?

Scratching the door is simply the dog's way of saying he wants to be with you. Avoid prolonged scratching by letting him in quickly, or, better still, when you see him approaching, open the door in advance if possible. To prevent a badly damaged door, tack a rubber mat to the spot he scratches, or install a pet door, which will allow him to come and go without troubling you in any way.

How much exercise (romping in the garden and/or walking on leash) does a grown dog need?

Size of Dog	Daily Exercise Time
Toy	20 minutes
Miniature (to 15 pounds)	30 minutes
16 – 35 pounds	45 minutes
36 – 60 pounds	1 hour
61 pounds and over	1 1/2 hours

Divide the daily total in half and exercise your dog in the morning and the evening. It is important to keep regular schedules, rain or shine. Do not exercise your dog for five minutes one day and three hours the next.

How can you give the dog plenty of exercise, keeping him confined at the same time?

Your dog should never be allowed to run loose, but you can give him maximum exercise by setting up a "runner." Place a sturdy leather leash on a new clothesline or long wire. Securely attach the line or wire, about 5 feet off the ground, to two sturdy trees or poles. Now the dog, wearing the leash, can run up and down as much as he likes. If he is unattended for a long time, make sure there is a shady place for him to rest in hot weather and a warm doghouse to shelter him during cold spells.

Your male dog wanders, sometimes disappearing for days. Where does he go?

He is probably wooing a female in heat. Try to locate the owner of the female and ask him to confine his pet during her heat period. If there are no bitches in the area, your pet may have joined a pack of dogs, or he may be visiting someone who keeps him confined. In any case, it is wise to fence your property or put your dog on a long leash or runner when he is exercised in the yard. A pet should always be under the control of his owner.

Your dog romps in the woods and comes back covered with burrs. How do you remove them?

Use the tines of an ordinary household fork to remove the burrs. Take care to find all of them. Check under and between his legs, in his paws, between his toes, and under his ear flaps.

When you remove your dog's leash, he races away. How can you catch him before he is out of sight?

Never allow your dog off his leash until he has learned to come when called. Do not give chase when he dashes off. He might think it's a game in which he's required to outrace you. Instead, call his name, tell him to "Come," then turn and walk in the opposite direction, looking back and continuing to call. When he returns, act friendly, even though you feel like wringing his neck. If you scold him, he will believe that his return has caused your anger and he won't rush back the next time you call.

The dog has started to chase cars and might get killed or cause an accident. How can you prevent this?

Put the choke collar and leash on the dog and take him out. When he lunges after a car, tug him back so that he stumbles. Say "B-a-d, b-a-d," and take him inside immediately. The physical punishment and the abrupt end to his walk will discourage the unwanted behavior. However, it will probably take several sessions before he entirely foregoes the joy of the chase.

Your dog refuses to ride on an escalator. What should you do?

Your dog should *never* be placed on an escalator. His claws can get caught in the machinery and rip from his paws. Either carry him, use the staircase, or find an elevator if possible.

What is the best way to get your dog into an elevator?

An automatic elevator can be lethal to your dog because his tail or leash can get caught between the closing doors. If it is essential that he travel by elevator, hold some learning sessions in an uncrowded one. When the door opens and he hesitates, push him forward and *enter behind him.* Now the dog will be safely inside, leaving you to cope with the closing doors.

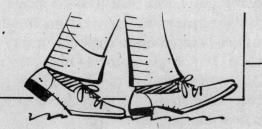

When you are shopping, is it wise to leave the dog outside the store, tied to a post? He receives many admiring pats and glances, and in return, wags his tail, behaving in a very friendly manner.

Thousands of animals are stolen every year, and your dog would probably put up very little resistance, so don't leave him unattended when you enter a store.

Is there any advantage in having your dog tattooed?

Tattooing provides identification and, therefore, extra protection for your pet. Use your social security number for the identifying mark and then list the number with the National Dog Registry, 227 Stebbins Road, Carmel, New York 10512. (The fee for the listing is nominal.) Humane societies and other professionals will usually look for such a marking on a lost dog, and if the animal is registered with the National Dog Registry and it is notified, your pet will be speedily returned to you. The tattoo is proof that the pet belongs to you and acts as a deterrent to thieves. If you sell your pet, the new owner must re-register the animal, adding an extra numeral and initial to the existing ones.

Who should tattoo the dog? Will it hurt him?

A veterinarian may perform the operation or recommend someone who is qualified. Fur is shaved from an ear or an area near the groin of the pet's right back leg, and an indelible figure is fixed upon the body under the skin. It sounds painful, but it is not. After the dog has been tattooed, keep the area free of hair so the identification number is in clear view.

Your dog jumps up and puts his paws on people's shoulders and you are afraid he might knock someone over. How can you stop him?

If you obtain your dog when he is a puppy, discourage the development of this habit. Otherwise, put the choke collar and leash on the dog and hold him. Ask a friend to enter the room. The minute the dog leaps forward, use the corrective jerk, say "B-a-d, b-a-d," and shake a noisemaker. Next, call the animal by his name and order him to "Sit." Praise him for obedience.

The regimental mascot, Culprit, once sniffed under the skirt of Queen Elizabeth II. If such a distinguished dog cannot be stopped from behaving in this way, what chance do you stand of correcting your dog?

Allow your dog to roam with his choke collar and leash attached. When he advances on a female visitor (or volunteer), catch hold of the leash and quickly give the corrective jerk, strongly say "B-a-d, b-a-d," and shake a noisemaker. In time, he will understand that this is a pleasantry he must forego.

The dog mounts other dogs and children, and he rubs against the legs of visitors. What should you do to stop this embarrassing behavior?

You should either give him plenty of exercise so he expends his excess energy or mate him. If these alternatives are not feasible, let him walk around with his choke collar and leash attached, and when he behaves improperly, use a severe corrective jerk and reprimand him, saying "B-a-d, b-a-d." If the oral command fails, shake the noisemaker. You've done this and he still misbehaves? Then permit the victim to push his/her knee or foot into the dog's chest, knocking him down. This method may sound harsh, but mounting is very unpleasant for the victim, and children can be traumatized when large dogs attack them in this manner.

Should you reprimand your dog for misbehaving when you were away from home?

No. He will not understand what he has done wrong, even if just a few minutes pass between the deadly deed and the reprimand. Your scolding will only make him nervous and confused, and he will think you are mistreating him. Try to catch him in the act, then use the "B-a-d" procedure.

Is it natural for children to handle pets with kindness?

Children often do not understand what behavior is considered kind or cruel. Therefore, you must teach them to be gentle, loving, and considerate with their pets.

Your child squeezes the dog tightly and pulls him by his tail. What should you do?

Excessive squeezing of the dog can injure his innards. It is also very painful, as is having his tail tugged. Do not permit your child to be alone with the dog until you are absolutely certain that the youngster can be trusted. If the cruelty persists, a new home must be found for the dog because the pet may retaliate and harm the child.

Can you teach your pup to protect your child?

When your pet is between one and two years old, he will automatically become protective, provided he and your child are already pals. My Golden Retriever walked me to school, which was 1/2 mile away, and without orders from anyone, brought me home again.

The neighborhood children want to ride on the back of your Old English Sheepdog, but you have forbidden them to try it. Are you being unreasonable?

As the owner of the dog, you make the rules. The animal's back could be injured, or he may be harshly kicked when someone tries to mount him. If a child has an accident, you might have to assume the medical costs. You might even be sued for damages. In any case, most dogs are not physically constructed to carry loads on their backs.

After the dog plays with the children next door, he seems disturbed. What could be the cause?

Without being observed, watch the children to see how they treat him. If you can't do this, upon the dog's return home, check his limbs and neck, looking for elastic or bits of string around them. Also examine his neck for inflammation or flesh cuts due to excessive pulling on his collar. If there is nothing physically wrong, the youngsters may merely make him nervous, and he might prefer not to play with them, or he may be overstimulated from the enjoyment, feeling depressed when obliged to return to a quieter atmosphere.

Your dog is usually very brave, but fireworks and thunderstorms frighten him. What can you do?

During a fireworks display, keep your dog on a leash and by your side. If he runs free, he may be injured by the explosives, or he may dart away when frightened. During thunderstorms, allow the dog to lie in a closet where he cannot see the lightning and where the thunder is less audible. Dogs who are sensitive about such things usually remain that way, so be kind and understanding.

Do dogs like people to scratch them?

If your dog is like most dogs, he will enjoy being gently scratched on the stomach and will roll over on his back to indicate that this is what he wants. Other sensitive spots are on his back where the tail joins the body, behind his ears, and under his chin. Some pets like to be scratched on the top of the head, while others are irritated by it.

Family Matters

- **Breeding Pedigreed Dogs**
- **Mating Your Female**
- **Inbreeding, Line Breeding, and Outbreeding**
- **Mating Your Male**
- **Stud Dogs**
- **Mating Problems**
- **Pregnancy**
- **The Whelping Box**
- **The Birth Process**
- **Arrival of the Pups**
- **Caring for the Mother and Offspring**
- **Orphan Puppies**
- **Weaning**
- **Docking Your Pup's Tail**
- **Cropping Your Pup's Ears**
- **Removing the Dewclaws**
- **Selling Your Litter**

Can you make a great deal of money breeding pedigreed dogs in your home?

Breeding requires capital for proper facilities to keep and display pups. Home-breeding from only one pet almost always results in financial losses, poor specimens, and disappointments. Eventually, the breeder runs out of space to accommodate the growing animals. The dogs get bigger and bigger and nobody comes to buy. In the end, the owner tries to give them away, but there are still no takers. For the average pet owner, it is probably best that he not get involved in the business of breeding.

What points should you consider before you mate your female?

Are you prepared to maintain *all* the pups your female produces for their entire lives? If not, what will you do with them? Where will they be housed? Can you afford to license them? Can you afford to feed them? To whom will you sell them? To whom will you give them away? (It is difficult to find homes for puppies even when you offer them freely.) If you are breeding your dog because you want a second pet, it is easier to purchase another one, and have your female spayed.

What is inbreeding? Line breeding? Outbreeding?

Inbreeding involves the breeding of closely related animals: brother and sister; mother and son. Line breeding involves the breeding of distantly related animals: half-brother and half-sister; grandparent and grandchild. Outbreeding involves breeding between two animals who have no common relative, but in some cases, a very remote family link may exist.

Are the offspring that result from inbreeding normal?

Inbreeding emphasizes defects as well as virtues. When carried out by experienced breeders, very fine specimens can be produced. However, too much inbreeding results in emotionally unstable pets. Therefore, inbreeding should only be performed by knowledgeable, professional breeders.

Why must your bitch be wormed before she is mated?

Worms can be transmitted to unborn pups, and those who do become infested have a poor chance of survival. If a bitch has already been mated, she can safely be wormed within the first two or three weeks of pregnancy.

The veterinarian says your female must be immunized against distemper and hepatitis a short time before mating. Why?

Your dog will pass the immunity along to her pups so there will be no chance for them to contract these deadly diseases before they receive their own vaccinations.

Should you mate your bitch during her first heat period?

At the time of her first heat period, your female will probably be too young to deal with the responsibilities of motherhood—pregnancy, whelping, and nursing. Let her enjoy her youth. If she is a small- to medium-size dog, wait until she is about 1 1/2 to 2 1/2 years old before mating her. If she is larger, wait until she is at least two years old.

Can your bitch be bred each time she is in heat?

She can be bred from her first heat to her last, but it is not wise. Excess breeding causes physical deterioration in the mother and weak puppies. Breeding once a year is sufficient, up to the age of seven or eight. The AKC refuses to register the litters of a dam who is twelve years of age or older.

Can the female become pregnant any time during the heat period?

No. During the first eight or nine days and between day fifteen and day twenty-one, she may reject the male. Between the tenth day and the fourteenth day, she will be very receptive and actually use extraordinary measures to escape confinement so she can go out and find a mate. A coupling during these crucial days will most likely result in a litter. It is usually obvious when her receptive period occurs. She will become extremely playful and flirtatious, inducing any available male to join her. Quite frequently, she will stand with legs outstretched and flag her tail (lifting it to one side or over her back) to provide ready access to her sex organs.

Your dog suffered severe pelvic injuries in a car accident. Can you still breed her?

Yes. But you probably shouldn't. It would be a good idea to have her spayed. Otherwise, she may become impregnated accidentally and then need a cesarean section to deliver her offspring.

What is the best age for a dog to sire a litter?

A dog may be as young as six months, but it is better to wait until he is more mature, about 1 to 1 1/2 years old. It is not a good idea for dogs over eleven years old to sire pups, and the AKC will not register the offspring of these dogs. So no matter how illustrious the strain, the pups will be worthless from a financial point of view.

Dogs in the same litter can have different fathers. True or False?

True. Of course, each individual pup has only one father, but a bitch who mates with two different males during her heat period may have some eggs fertilized by one male and some, by the other.

Your bitch had a brief sexual encounter with a mongrel, and it resulted in a litter. Will there be a little bit of mongrel in every pup she produces for the rest of her days?

No. If she has a future mating exclusively with a male of her breed, her pups will be of a pure strain.

Who supervises the mating?

Usually the owner of the male supervises the breeding, and the female is sent to him. One reason for this is because the male is more likely to be injured from the female's efforts to reject him. It is rare for the female to be harmed physically, although she may become nervous if it is a new experience. To ease her tension, accompany your female to the chosen location and bring her home again.

You can get a good stud without charge in exchange for the "pick of the litter." Is this a fair deal?

It is an economical way of arranging matters, but it has a serious drawback. The owner of the stud will probably select the very pup you want, and you will be legally bound to let him have it.

Isn't it stingy for the owner of a sire to charge for his dog's pleasure?

Owners of worthwhile stud dogs tend to invest a great deal of money in them. The animals are a result of many years of supervised scientific breeding, and the owner is being compensated for this very distinguished heritage, which is passed on to your dam's family. In addition, if there is a scuffle during a mating, it is usually the male who becomes injured.

Why is there a tremendous variation in stud fees?

The fee is based on hereditary factors and whether or not the dog is a Champion of his breed, on his experience in mating a dam, on the pups he has previously produced, and on the popularity of the breed. If these factors are on the plus side, he will command a higher fee.

What does "to approved bitches only" mean?

The stud's owner will not allow his male to fertilize any female he considers unsuitable by reason of pedigree, heredity, or conformation. In this way, the stud maintains his reputation as the father of high-quality pups.

Once your dog has experienced the joys of mating, he will always be restless, no longer your same lovable pet. True or False?

False! Mating has no effect on his relationships with humans, particularly those who feed, house, and cater to all his other needs.

How can you make sure the stud you choose is free of hip dysplasia?

Ask for a certificate from the Hip Dysplasia Control Registry. If this is unavailable, request that an X-ray be taken by a trusted veterinarian known to both parties. If neither of these suggestions is agreeable to the owner of the stud, find another sire.

You want to use a sire who lives far away. Can you send your bitch to him alone by plane?

This is not a good idea. The journey may upset your female, and she might become even more disturbed from the mating experience, especially if her owner is nowhere in sight. Either accompany your dog to her destination or find a sire closer to home.

You have a male offspring of a Champion sire and dam and would like to hire him out for breeding. How do you arrange this?

Attend dog shows and make contact with other breeders. Advertise in magazines or in the pet section of your local newspaper. Tell local veterinarians, animal hospitals, boarding kennels, and groomers that your dog is available for breeding (and return the favor by recommending their services).

Should you have a written agreement with the owner of the sire? If so, how should it be worded?

If the sire's owner has a prepared form, read it carefully before signing it. If not, write an informal letter and include the following: 1. If a litter does not result from the first mating, a second mating will be provided, free of charge, the next time the dam is in heat. 2. State the fee that the owner is to receive and how and when it is to be paid. 3. When a "pick of the litter" agreement replaces a monetary fee, state that the sire's owner must make his selection before the pups are seven weeks old. (Otherwise, you will not be able to part with a single animal until he has made his choice. This may seriously reduce your selling opportunities.) 4. If the male is injured during the mating, even as a result of your female's behavior, state that you are not responsible for any damages.

Your female pursues a male, but when he tries to mount her, she squeals, snaps at him, and leaps away. Why?

This is probably either her first or at least an early mating and she is frightened. If the male is inexperienced, the situation becomes more difficult. Discouraged by the bitch's snapping and growling, the male might run away. In this case, grip the female's body, preventing her escape, and muzzle her to make sure she doesn't bite you or the male. It is better, however, to use a veteran stud. He will be able to cope with the female and you will avoid a forced mating.

Can you help the dogs have a successful mating?

Don't do anything if they are getting along without you. However, if the bitch is obviously in a flirtatious mood and the male is sexually aroused and attempts to mount her but has difficulty keeping her in position, have the bitch's owner hold the female's head steady with one hand, supporting her under the abdomen with the other hand. This will prevent the bitch from sitting or moving forward when the male grips her body with his forepaws.

If the male has a firm hold on the bitch but cannot enter, maneuver her rear to ease entry.

If a problem arises because the dogs' heights vary greatly, place a blanket under the hind paws of the shorter animal.

If the floor is slippery, causing the male to slip backward or the female to glide forward, position them on rubber matting.

If the male tires because of many unsuccessful attempts, let him rest. Stroke his back, and stroke the female near the spot where her tail joins her back. Do not become angry or impatient. Reassure them in gentle tones.

If entry seems impossible, the female may require dilation of the vagina, which must be performed by a veterinarian.

If you must assist your pet, be careful. Keep your face out of biting distance because your own dog may attack you in frustration or fear.

Is it true that during a successful mating, the male and female become locked together?

Yes. This tie occurs during copulation. The male's penis has a knoblike enlargement at the base, which becomes engorged with blood during the mating act, making it impossible for him to withdraw from the female. Most breeders believe that a tie lasting less than fifteen to twenty minutes will be unfruitful, although pups are sometimes conceived. Once this tie has been established, both animals should be comforted and held, preventing a struggle to disengage, which may injure the male, and preventing the female from biting the male. The sire can be trapped in the tie for as long as an hour.

Your bitch has been mated twice, but no pups were conceived. What is wrong?

She may have worm infestation, a hormonal imbalance, a vitamin deficiency, or she just might be too run-down to conceive. A physical defect such as cysts in the ovaries could prevent conception too. Have your female checked by a veterinarian. If nothing seems wrong, perhaps the mating did not occur on her most fertile days. Try again, repeating the mating two additional times during the same heat period.

How can you tell when the bitch has actually conceived?

About a month after the mating, your bitch may look more rounded and her appetite might increase substantially. But these signs don't always appear. Usually about six weeks after conceiving, definite lumps can be felt in her lower abdomen, but it is unwise to poke around to find them. The safest way to tell if your female is pregnant is to take her to the vet, and he will check for pups' heartbeats.

What is a false pregnancy?

The female acts as if she is going to become a mother because of a hormonal imbalance. Her mammary glands frequently fill with milk, and she mothers toys and other animals. To save her from this anguish, it is best to have her spayed early on, unless, of course, you want to breed her.

Should a pregnant female have more exercise, less exercise, or no exercise?

She should be walked every day, but do not allow her to romp about. And most important, do not let her run around in circles. The unborn pups may move into an awkward position, resulting in a difficult delivery.

How long after mating will the puppies be born?

The period of gestation varies from sixty-one days to sixty-five days. If the pups are not born within this period, bring the dam to the vet, especially if she seems distressed. A pup may be stuck or may have died in the birth canal.

Are Bulldog pups difficult to deliver?

Yes. Bulldogs are among the breeds which have large, square heads, making delivery more difficult. Generally, a cesarean section is required. Consult your veterinarian about this in advance. He may prefer to have your female on his premises at the time she goes into labor.

How do you make a whelping box?

You will need a box large enough to accommodate the mother when she is fully stretched out on her side with several inches to spare on all sides. Three sides of the box should be very high (12 to 18 inches), and the fourth side should be low enough for the bitch to step out whenever she chooses. Make the box very comfortable, layering the bottom with plenty of toweling (which can be destroyed or washed) over her regular mattress. It is a good idea to secure all the padding with safety pins at the sides and corners so the pups cannot crawl in between and suffocate. The box, and the room in which it is placed, should be about 70°F. Test the temperature in the room at floor level where the box is situated.

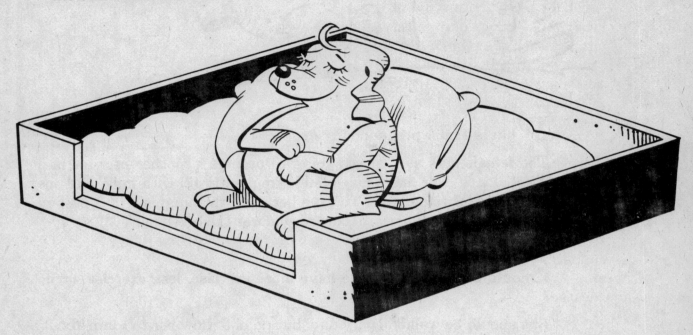

How can you make sure the mother will have her babies in the whelping box and not someplace of her own choosing?

About three weeks before the pups are due, place the mother's regular bedding into the whelping box and encourage her to sleep there. By the time she is ready to become a mother, she will be familiar with the whelping box, recognizing it as a natural place to deliver her pups.

What items will you need for the arrival of the new pups?

You will need plenty of newspaper and some old towels for drying the newborns, providing extra bedding, and wiping dirt off the pups or the dam. Have your first-aid kit handy. And it never hurts to have a bottle of brandy nearby. You can use a very minute drop for a failing pup or a slightly larger dose (1/4 teaspoon to 1/2 jigger) for your dam (according to her weight) to ease her discomfort.

Will the mother protect the pups with her body, or should you put warm blankets in the whelping box?

The mother will usually protect and warm her babies by pushing them into the middle of the whelping box and curving her body around them. If you provide loose blankets, make sure they are very small. She will paw them to make a nest for her offspring. Always check that the pups don't get caught underneath the blankets. If they do, they might suffocate. (For this reason, some people feel shredded newspaper is safer.)

Your bitch is almost due to give birth, but her teats are not very prominent. Should you worry?

Yes. Newborn pups must nurse immediately after they are born. About a week before whelping time, massage the teats regularly with some mineral oil, pulling each one gently as you do.

Should you help the mother whelp her pups?

Give her verbal reassurance, but do not touch her unless it is absolutely necessary. Allow her a good deal of privacy even though you will be standing nearby. If the delivery is normal, she will not need any help. Instinct will see her through.

PRIVACY PLEASE

How do you know when it's time for your female to give birth?

Her temperature will drop to about 100°F. or less. She will probably stop eating and pace restlessly. She may ask to be let outside, then immediately come back in again. While outside, she may dig a hole. Indoors, she will gather newspaper, cloth, and anything else she can pile into a heap. Put her into the whelping box. When she gets out and has had a few minutes to stretch her limbs, put her back. Never leave her outdoors unattended. She and her pups might be harmed if she goes into labor under a rose bush or some other shrubbery, and you will not be able to move her until the delivery is over.

How long does labor last?

Three or four hours is usually the normal period when five or six puppies are born. In larger litters, the early pups may arrive between fifteen and thirty minutes apart, but later pups may arrive as long as one or two hours apart. The entire process should not take longer than twenty hours, no matter how many births are involved.

What happens during birth?

Usually the bitch lies on her side and you can observe contractions that cause her to pant. Her face bears signs of pain. After a while, she flips up her tail and a gush of clear, warm fluid is discharged, followed by a wriggling pup in a cloudy membranous sac. A cord with a wine or purple mass attached to it is expelled next. The cord is the umbilical cord; the mass is the placenta. The mother immediately curves her body into a circle, nips off the sac with her teeth and cuts the cord. She then nuzzles the newborn pup, licking him dry with her tongue, and pushes him toward a nipple for his first meal. Finally, she will eat the afterbirth if you do not remove it.

Must the dam eat all of the placentas?

No. She need not consume any, but if this is what she wants, do not stop her. Three or four placentas, however, is the limit. Remove the other ones if she doesn't raise objections and discard them. They will only give her diarrhea and bowel cramps.

What are some *dos* and *don'ts* during a normal delivery?

Do keep a record of the number of placentas expelled as follows:

Arrival of Pup 1 _____,   Arrival of Placenta 1 _____;

Arrival of Pup 2 _____,   Arrival of Placenta 2 _____;

and so on. Don't rely on memory because something may distract you. Each pup must be followed by his placenta. If, for some reason, there are less placentas than pups, call the vet to inject the dam with the proper medication, which will force the release of the residue. If it is left inside, the dam will die. Don't be too eager assisting a pup who is arriving in a natural fashion. Don't wash the bitch after she has finished whelping. This may cause infection, so let her wash herself. And *never* reach inside the female's vulva to try to remove anything.

Should newborn pups remain with the bitch while other pups are still being born?

It is advisable to have a second box lined with clean towels and slightly warmed by a heating pad. When the bitch goes into labor again, place the newly born pups, handling them very, very gently, in the box until she completes this delivery. Then bring the pups back to her. Otherwise, their absence will disturb her.

What events are *not* normal during birth?

Labor continuing for over an hour without the first pup arriving may indicate that he is in an incorrect position, blocking his and the other pups' passage. Call a vet immediately.

If you can see a puppy emerging but he is not quickly expelled, use a very clean cloth to hold him *gently* and help him out *very slowly* in rhythm with his mother's contractions.

If a pup is emerging tail first, do nothing unless there is difficulty. If there is excessive delay, grasp him with a cloth and assist in the delivery in coordination with the female's contractions.

If the placenta breaks, the pup will die when not whelped immediately. Don't panic. Very *gently* and *slowly*, remove him from the dam.

If the pup arrives in his sac but the female makes no attempt to free the confined puppy, quickly break the sac and remove the pup from the membrane. Otherwise, he will suffocate.

If the mother fails to sever the umbilical cord, or is a short-faced breed and cannot manage to do it unaided, cut the cord about 1 to 1 1/2 inches from the pup's navel.

If the newborn pup does not breathe, clear his mouth of mucus and breathe into it continually while rubbing his chest gently. Also move his limbs back and forth. If these methods fail, give his tail a tweak. He might jerk his limbs and begin breathing or yelping, or he may not respond at all. If he doesn't respond, there is nothing more you can do.

If the bitch fails to dry off her newborn pup by licking him and does not push him into feeding position, dry the pup with a clean cloth. Then place him with his mouth against a milk-filled nipple.

How do you know when the birth process is over?

It is sometimes difficult to tell when delivery has been completed. However, if the bitch appears tranquil, no contractions are observable, no lumps can be detected in her abdomen, and she laps a bowl of milk you offer her, you can be almost certain that it is over.

Is there something you should do for the mother after she has finished giving birth?

She won't like to leave her new pups, but take her out for a very short walk. (While she is out of the box, have someone clean it up, placing new towels over a comfortable cushioning.) If her coat is messy, wipe it with a sponge, and brush and comb her quickly. Give her a bowl of warm milk (or beef broth) and a bowl of water. However, stay with her while she drinks and do not leave the bowls near the pups. A new pup, crawling around blindly, may drown himself.

Do some breeds produce more pups in each litter? Which parent influences the number?

Toys usually produce two or three pups, medium-size dogs sometimes have as many as fifteen, and giant breeds quite frequently parent twenty in each litter. Most of the time more male pups are produced than females. Although the sire releases millions of sperm cells, he can only fertilize the amount of ripe egg cells the dam produces. Therefore, the dam is responsible for the size of the litter.

Are puppies born blind?

Yes. They will not be able to see for about two weeks, and even then, their eyes will appear to be blue and will be quite weak. To protect their vision, keep the pups away from strong sun or electric light for at least a month after they are born.

Are puppies born without ear openings?

By the time the pups reach two weeks of age, their ear canals will have opened. After the pups are four weeks old, test their hearing. Clap your hands to see if their attention is attracted. If a pup does not respond, remove him from the others and clap your hands several times. If he still fails to take notice, he is deaf. Professional breeders do not allow deaf pups to live.

Are pups born with their permanent teeth?

When your pups are eight weeks old, they will have their baby teeth. These are very sharp and tiny. At fifteen weeks, these teeth will loosen and begin to fall out. Their adult set—forty-two strong teeth—start to develop, and by the time the animals are six months old, their new teeth will all be in place.

Is it possible to tell if any members of the litter are born with defects?

Yes. A pup born with a harelip or a cleft palate is unable to nurse, and in his efforts to suck, he seriously upsets the mother. These malformations are considered legitimate grounds for destroying the pup immediately.

You were told that your litter needs "culling" because some of the pups have birth defects. What does this term mean?

Culling merely means weeding out the unhealthy specimens and putting them to death. Ask your veterinarian if this is the only option for your sickly pups. (Some breeders put their pups to sleep when the dam has an extremely large litter, which, in their opinion, she cannot feed, or when they cannot find homes for them.)

Should your female wear a collar when she is looking after a litter?

A tiny pup might get his paw caught in his mother's collar, and be unable to free himself. Therefore, remove the collar before she gives birth. She should not wear a flea collar because one of the pups may suck on it, releasing chemicals that can kill him.

Your female picks up her pups and hides them when you enter her room. Why?

She wants and needs privacy. If you continue to approach her, she may bare her teeth and actually bite you, especially if you try to pick up one of her pups. However, when they are about six weeks old, you and others can visit frequently. At this age, the puppies will be stronger and less susceptible to chills and germs, and the mother will be more relaxed.

Should the dam be fed extra meals after her litter is born?

The dam will usually ask for more food if you do not give it to her after her litter is born. She will now require about four feedings instead of the customary one or two. Double her normal amount of fresh or commercially prepared meat and increase her milk serving. (A 35-pound dog should have about 1 pint of whole milk each day.)

How warm should the room be for a litter of pups?

If the pups become chilled, they will die, no matter how hard you try to save them. For the first two to three weeks, the room occupied by the dam and her pups must be kept at a *constant* 75°F. (Buy a portable heater if you want to conserve fuel.) Check the overall room temperature and take a reading at floor level where the pups are kept. If there is a draft from a door, seal the bottom with a blanket and place a heating pad, set on "Low," underneath the whelping box. There should be some ventilation in the room, so do not block out every bit of fresh air. *Do not use a gas oven to provide heat.* It produces carbon monoxide, which can be fatal to the pups and make the dam ill.

When can you handle the newborn pups?

When the pups' eyes open, you can pet them. Place the pup on your lap and stroke him gently. Do not walk around with him. If the dam resents the intrusion, you will have to wait until she approves, which will probably be during the weaning period. Remember, a pup can die if he doesn't receive the proper amount of rest or is late in getting to his mother's teat. So do not handle the puppies excessively.

Should the dam spend all her time with the pups?

As long as she does not ignore her pups for too long, it is quite all right if she spends a little time with you. Her visit gives her a break from prodding and nursing pups who are constantly crawling under and over her. Treat her in your usual affectionate manner, but if you think she is over-staying her time, walk her back to the whelping box. If she comes in unexpectedly, check the litter in case she is trying to tell you that something is wrong.

How often does the whelping box need to be cleaned?

Clean it thoroughly at least once a day. Otherwise, it will smell bad. (Move the pups into another warm box when you are cleaning.) Always pad the bottom of the whelping box with plenty of newspaper, which can be removed, one or two sheets at a time, as they become soiled. When adding to existing paper, place the new sheets *underneath*, removing the old sheets from the top. And keep the entire room disinfected at all times.

What is "eclampsia"? What are its symptoms? How do you prevent your bitch from getting it?

Eclampsia is a rapid loss in calcium, which sometimes occurs when pups are nursing. The symptoms are a wild-eyed expression, panting, shaking, rigidity of muscles, and other signs of convulsions. A veterinarian must be called. He will give your female injections for a quick and complete recovery. (Some people believe that attacks often occur after loud noises or traumatic disturbances startle a sensitive bitch.)

How many nipples should a dam have? Do they all give milk?

The dam should have ten nipples. However, the first two closest to her front legs rarely contain much milk. If you have more than eight pups fighting for a nipple, rotate the pups, ensuring that each gets his fair share of mother's milk. And if two unlucky pups choose the first two nipples, move them to others. It is extremely important that you supervise the feedings so that all the offspring are nourished equally.

What is "mastitis"?

Mastitis is an infection of the teats, which become inflamed and swollen while the dam is nursing. She will be sick and in pain, and the pups will become very ill if they drink the milk. Usually the pups don't like the taste, a sure sign that something is wrong. Seek medical advice immediately.

What should you do if the dam has many, many more pups than teats?

Separate the litter into two sets, each set containing a maximum of eight pups. In the morning, allow the first set to drink the dam's milk while you feed the second set with warm milk from an eyedropper. Gently insert the dropper into the pup's mouth, then slowly squeeze the bulb to produce one tiny drop. (The pup will choke on too much milk, and he may draw it into his lungs and contract pneumonia.) Approximately two fillings of the eyedropper will satisfy a 5-ounce pup for two hours. (As the pups grow, use a bottle instead of the dropper, increasing the amount of milk.) At the next feeding, the first set will be fed with the dropper and the second set with their mother's milk, and so on. To identify the sets correctly, cut a small piece of fur off the rumps of members of the second set.

The puppies are tearing the dam's flesh. What should you do?

Your puppies are probably three weeks old with nails like sharp needles. When they put their front paws against the dam's stomach to nurse, they tear her skin. Lay each puppy on your lap on his back. Using ordinary sharp scissors, cut the white upper part of every nail. Make sure you do not cut the pink lower portion, which will cause pain and bleeding that is difficult to stop. Repeat the procedure about every eight days.

The dam dangles the pup from her mouth. Is this the way she should carry him?

Yes. She picks up the pup by the back of his neck and holds him firmly between her teeth. But when you pick up a pup, make sure both hands are placed around his body as you lift him.

Your puppies twitch. Is something wrong?

If they fail to twitch, it often means they are underfed or anemic. The twitching is just a passing phase.

How can you tell if the litter has worms?

Take a stool sample from one of the pups and give it to the veterinarian for testing. If one pup has worms, the entire litter is infected. The vet will provide you with medication and tell you when and how to give it. When the wormed pups eliminate on their papers, gather the papers and burn them. (Some worm diseases can be transmitted to humans.) After a couple of weeks, take another stool sample to the vet. It should show that the pup, and therefore all his brothers and sisters, is free of the parasite. Keep a record of wormings, medications used, and the veterinarian's name. This information should be given to anyone who purchases a pup from you.

Are pups immune to everything to which the dam is immune?

As long as the pups drink their mother's milk, they will remain immune to everything that she has been inoculated against. When the pets begin a new feeding schedule, they should be vaccinated against distemper. (About four weeks of age is a good time for the initial shots.) At fourteen weeks old, the puppies can receive their permanent shots for distemper, leptospirosis, and hepatitis. Boosters should be given every year thereafter.

Should pups be inoculated against heartworm?

Inoculation against heart-worm can be given when the pups are six weeks old. Your veterinarian will advise you.

Can you raise the pups if the dam dies while giving birth?

A dam rarely dies at this time. But if she should, the ideal solution is to find a foster mother with plenty of milk. If the pups are quite small, a cat is a suitable mother substitute. To make the foster mother adopt her new family, squeeze out some of her milk and smear it on the pups. Then the newcomers will smell familiar, and she may lick and fuss over them just as if they were her own. If she dislikes the pups, place them with her for nursing only, removing them afterward so she cannot harm them.

If a foster parent is unavailable, you will have to take care of the pups. Place them in a small cardboard carton lined on the bottom with a heating pad switched to "Low." Over the pad, place layers of newspaper covered with small towels (or blankets cut to size). The temperature at floor level and generally throughout the room *must* be 90°F. to 85°F. during the first week, 85°F. to 80°F. during the second week, 80°F. to 75°F. during the third week, and 75°F. to 70°F. during the fourth week. The orphans need to be fed every three hours, day and night, until they are ten days old with one of the commercial products especially formulated for weaning pups. Use an eye-dropper, feeding the fluid to each pup, drop by drop. (A tube for feeding is also available. It is pushed down the pup's throat and into his stomach.)

Unfortunately, newborns need help to urinate and defecate. So roll each pup over and over after every feeding. Do this very gently, and massage under the pup's tail and between his hind legs. If the puppy whimpers at any time, this rolling and massaging is probably what he needs.

Because the pups cannot benefit from prolonged immunity to disease from their natural mother's milk, keep the box and the pups very, very clean, and speak to your vet about an early vaccination schedule.

Caring for the pups by yourself is an around-the-clock job. You will have accomplished a great feat if the entire litter survives.

Your mother dog ate excrement after her pups were born. Is this normal?

It is an inborn trait but she could get very sick, so remove anything dirty, wet, or soiled immediately.

Should your pups' tails be "docked"?

Docking is cutting the tails so that they conform to the length specified by the AKC. Before you bring the pups to the vet to have this minor operation performed, check the breed standard for your pet. Do not leave the length decision to the vet because the tails can't be stuck back on again if he makes them too short. Docking should be done when the pups are four to seven days old. Sometimes there is much bleeding, so make sure the dam does not lick the stumps, preventing healing.

Are you supposed to have the dog's dewclaws removed?

It is not necessary to have these two claws (situated on the inside of the hind legs) removed, and for St. Bernards, Great Pyrenees, and Briards, they are considered to be part of the breed's beauty. Although the dewclaws are not useful, they do not do any harm. However, if the dog is to be kept for hunting or working purposes, the dewclaws might rip off when he is performing some of his tasks. The operation is usually performed at the same time the puppies' tails are docked.

Should you crop your dog's ears?

Several breeds, including the Doberman Pinscher, usually have their ears cropped to meet breed standards. A section of the ear is removed to form a sharp triangular point. Most owners crop their dog's ears because it enhances their pet's appearance, but it is considered a cruel practice in England and was banned in 1974. The operation must be performed by a veterinarian when the pet is under anesthesia. The best time for this procedure is when the pup is about eight weeks old.

Fighting breaks out among members of the litter. How do you handle this?

Some breeders believe this fighting should be ignored because it is a natural part of the growing-up process. Unless larger pups are attacking smaller ones, endangering the smaller pups' health, it is not necessary to intervene. You might want to separate the large from the small pups between feeding times (the hours when they become mischievous because they have nothing else to do). If fighting still breaks out, at least it's an even battle. Or you can remove the bullies, letting them play together, while the undersized pet remains with those who are gentler and nearer his own size. But do not leave the small pet totally by himself. It will not be good for his emotional development.

When can pups be weaned?

Puppies may be weaned when they are four weeks old. Proceed in the following way:

• *Day 1:* Prepare a sufficient quantity of commercial puppy formula, heating it slightly so that it is lukewarm. Pour it into aluminum pie dishes and take each pup and push his mouth into the mixture. He will resist, splashing formula all over, but eventually he may take one or two laps. Work with another pup, and another, keeping them in a row alongside the necessary amount of pie dishes. Then return them to their mother. Later the same day, repeat the process.

• *Day 2:* Repeat the procedure three times. You will probably have better results.

• *Day 3:* Repeat as in Day 2.

• *Day 4 to Day 28:* Provide four feedings, adding some dry baby cereal to the formula. Keep the pups from nursing, but allow them to sleep with their mother. As the pups become accustomed to their meals, they will go to the dam less often for milk. This will cause her supply to dry up as it should.

• *Fifth week:* Gradually add to their food top-quality raw chopped meat from the butcher or commercially packaged food consisting of meat, cheese, and essential nutrients recommended for their age group. The pups may resist the new mix, so offer encouragement by putting little dabs on your finger, holding it out to each pup. Once one braves the new taste, the others will follow. Supply a *shallow* dish of water and invite the pups to lap from it.

• *Sixth week:* When the pups are eating a substantial quantity of meat, change their routine to two meat meals and two formula/cereal meals a day. Make sure drinking water is always available.

• *Seventh week:* Gradually substitute the raw meat (or the meat-cheese commercial mix) with commercial dog food consisting of chewy, tender pieces of beef. Continue until the dog is completely on commercial dog food. Also, slowly reduce feedings to two meals a day, one in the morning and one at night.

Can you feed your dog on table scraps instead of commercial dog food?

Dogs fed on table scraps are not usually as healthy as dogs who are given commercial dog food. Commercial food companies are continually working on special formulas that contribute to the dog's good bone development and shiny coat, and provide the animal with well-balanced meals. Table scraps or meals you might prepare just for your dog cannot compete with commercial food. In addition, if your pet becomes a finicky eater, it will be difficult to leave him with friends, and he may refuse to eat when left in a kennel or hospital.

Should the pups eat and drink from the same plate?

Usually there is a lot of jostling when all the pups are eating from the same dish, so make sure each gets his fair share. If you give a pup his own dish, he will take his time eating because he will not have to compete with his littermates for food, and his digestion will benefit. Still, a greedy brother or sister may gobble up his own food and start on the meal of a slower neighbor. It is necessary, therefore, to keep an eye on all the pups at feeding time.

Your dam spit up some food and then encouraged the pups to eat it. Why?

This is a natural tendency. When dogs were wild, the mother hunted for her food. Chewing the meat and spitting it up was her way of providing her pups with nourishment. Today, it is neither necessary for her to hunt nor to throw up. If you are not already giving the pups meat, this is the signal that it is time to do so.

Your pups have loose bowel movements. Can you prevent this?

Loose bowel movements usually occur when there is a change in food or in the number of feedings. This is because the pets' bowels are very sensitive. If you are giving your pups whole milk, substitute skimmed milk, and if they are over five weeks old, stop the milk completely, supplying water instead. And when mixing their food, use less water, keeping it fairly dry.

When can the pups go outdoors?

They can experience their first taste of fresh air, sunshine, and outdoor scents at six weeks of age. Before this, however, the temperature in their room should gradually be lowered to 70°F. If the sun is shining, let them out for a short time, but if it is cool, have them poke their noses out for just a couple of minutes. Keep them indoors during icy cold, rainy, or windy weather. Do not let them lie in scorching sunshine. This is just as bad as exposure to extreme cold.

What steps do you take to sell your litter?

If the owner of the sire has "pick of the litter," ask him to make his selection first. Then decide if you wish to keep a pup or two. Post bulletins in your neighborhood or place an ad in your local newspaper, giving a telephone number only. If you wish to use a regional or national magazine, send in the ad as soon as you are sure that the pups are healthy. Include the date of birth of the pups, your address, and telephone number.

Is it necessary to register the litter with the AKC?

If the litter is a result of a mating between a registered stud and bitch, it is a good idea to register the litter with the AKC. Registered pups will command a higher price, and registration papers are proof of your litter's elite ancestry. With the sale of each pup, give the buyer an individual litter registration application (the AKC will send you these once they have registered the entire litter).

When the prospective buyer has selected a pup, what do you do?

Provide the buyer with a box or suitable container lined with soft material to protect the pup on his journey. If the buyer wants to come back for the pet, ask for a deposit and in his presence cut an identifying mark in the dog's fur. Keep a record sheet of all financial transactions and identifying marks.

How young can the pup be when you sell him?

A pup should be at least eight weeks old before he goes to his new home. At that time, he will be ready to face the new challenge.

What information does the buyer need?

Supply written instructions on feeding and records of wormings and vaccinations (type of vaccine and date given). Also provide an application for AKC membership if necessary. Emphasize that the pup should never be disturbed while sleeping or eating, and that he should not be handled too much. Assure the buyer you will provide any information he needs if he has questions later on. It is very important to create a good image if you plan to breed again. And if it is your only litter, you will want to feel satisfied that all your pups went to good homes.

On the Road

- **Boarding Kennels**
- **Preparing Your Pet for Kennel Life**
- **Friends as "Dog-Sitters"**
- **Hospital Boarding**
- **Interstate Travel**
- **Overseas Travel**
- **Traveling by Plane**
- **Traveling by Train**
- **Traveling by Bus**
- **Car Travel**
- **Traveling with Several Dogs**
- **Highway Accidents**

How far in advance should you book your pet into a boarding kennel?

If the kennels in your area tend to become crowded, make the necessary arrangements for your pet before you pay in advance for your vacation. At the very least, book his accommodations six weeks before your departure.

Is it better to leave your pet with relatives or friends when you go on vacation?

Your pet is going to live for many years, and you will probably take quite a few trips during his lifetime. The goodwill of relatives and neighbors can easily be exhausted, and they may unknowingly disregard or neglect your pet during your absence. Select a reliable boarding kennel, run by experienced people who will know exactly what to do no matter what arises. Try to accustom the pet to boarding-kennel life at an early age.

How do you prepare your pet for the kennel?

Take him to the kennel and leave him there overnight. Some time later, take him there for a weekend or two. Then, when you leave for your longer vacation, he will be familiar with the people and the environment.

These short stays also provide you with the chance to see if you like the facilities and the kind of care that is provided. If you dislike something, you will have an opportunity to discuss it with the owner before you go away for an extended period, and you will feel secure in the knowledge that your pet is being treated properly while you are gone.

Is it a good idea to leave your dog with someone who has a cat?

You will certainly save a large sum of money in kennel fees. Try it for one or two weekends first. If the pets like each other and your friend understands the dog's needs, which are different from a cat's, there shouldn't be any problems.

Is it better to leave your dog in a luxurious kennel?

Many palatial boarding kennels are franchised operations run by business people. They may not pay attention to your pet's emotional needs, spending more of their time serving fancy diets in elaborate dishes, or tending to colorful carpets, private air-landing strips, daily medical check-ups, and other "trimmings" that are not necessary. Instead, locate a long-established owner-operated kennel, where the owner lives on or near the premises. Your dog should receive loving care, an extremely important consideration at a time of separation.

What features do you look for when selecting a kennel?

An owner-operated kennel is nearly always best, especially if the owner is available round-the-clock. Does the owner seem kind, compassionate, and knowledgeable? Are the cages clean? Are occupants perky and well groomed? Do the number of cages correspond to the number of exercise runs? Ask if your pet must have had his DHL (distemper, hepatitis, and leptospirosis) shots before being accepted. If the owner insists upon them, you know he is taking suitable health precautions, not only for your dog but for all the others as well! When you are looking at kennels, do not make an appointment in advance. Just drop in. That way, owners cannot make special preparations for your visit and give you a false picture of kennel life.

Your dog is very attached to you. Do you think he might die if you leave him in a kennel?

During his early training, say to your pet, "I am coming back," and give him a loving pat or hug. Then go out. When you return, say "I'm home," and make a big fuss over him. In time, he will understand that when these words are spoken, you are leaving but will be back again. He may respond by putting his ears back or looking forlorn. In any event, encourage calm behavior and no excessive barking. When you take him to the kennel, tell him you are coming back, give him his usual farewell gesture, and go. Do not cry or show signs that this time is different from the other times when you left him behind. Healthy dogs rarely die in reliable kennels. In fact, they often enjoy the change.

Do you need any special documentation when you book your pet in a kennel?

Take the dog's vaccination papers certifying that he has had shots for distemper, hepatitis, and leptospirosis. If your dog is old or has a terminal illness, write instructions for the kennel owner, outlining the steps to be taken if the pet should die while you are away. If you do not do this, the kennel owner must keep the body in cold storage until you return.

The proprietor of the kennel has instructed you to leave family members home when you drop the dog off. Why?

Sometimes during a big farewell scene, the dog imagines that a great tragedy has occurred, and he becomes very frightened. Take him by yourself; say good-bye quickly, lovingly, and cheerfully, and he won't be disturbed.

Your dog is very frail. Should you leave him at a boarding kennel?

If a regular boarding kennel knows your dog is sickly, they can refuse to accept him. Bring your pet to an animal hospital that also boards, and supply a list of his ailments, including any allergies he might have to drugs or food.

Should you board your dog in a hospital so that a veterinarian will be close by if your pet becomes ill?

If your dog is suffering from a chronic complaint that might flare up any time, it is wise for him to be near medical assistance. However, if he is perfectly healthy, it is best not to board him in a hospital where sick animals enter and leave constantly. The hospital employees can carry germs on their clothing and hands, inadvertently infecting your pet. In addition, dogs are subject to certain illnesses in which the germs are airborne, infecting the animal even if he doesn't come in contact with a carrier.

Will your dog mix with other animals while he is a boarder?

Some kennels are very strict about keeping animals apart, but others allow them to mingle, believing that the pets will enjoy playmates. You must decide what your pet will like best.

The boarding kennel owner insisted that you pick up your dog on the date you specified. She said it may upset your pet if you return later than expected. Why?

A pet, especially one accustomed to being boarded, associates certain activities with your return. Perhaps his name card is taken off his cage, or his run is fumigated. His identification collar may be replaced by his street collar. A sensitive dog interprets these happenings, and when you don't arrive, he is heartbroken.

You have two dogs. Should you board them in the same place?

If they enjoy each other's company at home, they will probably prefer being together. So book them in the same kennel.

What will happen if you leave your pet for months at a time?

When a dog is left with another person for a long period of time, he very often transfers his affections and has little or no interest in his original owner upon his return. Although you may think your pet is pining away for you, he may actually be replacing an old love with a new one.

140

Can you transport your dog from state to state without government interference?

The Interstate Commerce Commission governs the movement of livestock, and some states have strict regulations regarding animals who enter and leave their territory. Therefore, it is vital that you have in your possession the following papers: *a valid license, an up-to-date health certificate,* and *a current rabies vaccination certificate.*

These are regulation forms that will be provided by the licensing authority and/or your veterinarian. Make sure you have the vet's signature, the correct spelling of his name, and his full address on these forms. Then you will be set to travel anywhere in the United States (*mainland* only) and Canada.

Are there hotels and motels that accept dogs?

Yes! There are over 8,000 of these establishments and they are listed in a book called *Touring with Towser,* which can be obtained for a nominal fee from Gaines Dog Research Center, 250 North Street, White Plains, New York 10602.

Does your dog need a passport to travel overseas?

He does not need a passport with a picture attached as you do, but he does need up-to-date papers:

- *Current license.*

- *Shippers Export Declaration* form (which can be provided by your travel agent or the line transporting the animal).

- *Rabies Vaccination Certificate* from an official veterinarian confirming that the dog has been vaccinated within a certain number of days prior to departure (the required number of days varies from country to country).

- *Veterinary Health Certificate* from an official veterinarian declaring that the animal is not suffering from any contagious disease and has not been in contact with one, stating the type of vaccine used to protect him against distemper, and confirming he is in general good health.

Authentication of all these documents is necessary. It is done by the United States Department of Agriculture in your state. Also, the seal of the consulate general of the country or countries to be visited must be affixed to all of the documents before your pet departs from the United States. When you obtain the seal from the consulate, confirm that all arrangements are in order and ask if any new regulations have recently gone into effect. Make sure the forms are complete, that no questions have been left unanswered, and that signatures and titles are legible. If you cannot read the name of any signatory, request that the correct spelling be printed underneath.

Which countries are easy to enter with a dog?

The following lands are not considered too difficult to enter with your dog: Argentina, Austria, Bahamas, Belgium, Brazil, Canada, France, Greece, Guatemala, Holland, Israel, Italy, Luxembourg, Mexico, Netherlands Antilles, Philippines, Puerto Rico, Spain, Switzerland, Turkey, Venezuela, Virgin Islands.

The countries listed below require a long quarantine period and a great deal of extra papers and examinations (some absolutely refuse to admit animals): Australia, Bermuda, Denmark, England, Finland, Hawaii, Iceland, India, Ireland, Jamaica, Japan, New Zealand, Norway, Portugal, South Africa, Sweden, Vietnam, West Indies.

England requires that your dog, upon arrival from the United States, go into quarantine for six months. If you wish to avoid this separation, bring your animal to France first. But, before traveling, check the information bureaus of the countries you wish to visit for their up-to-date regulations.

Do cruise liners allow dogs on board?

Cruise liners do not allow animals on board. There is one ocean-going vessel that will accommodate your animal when it is making trans-Atlantic crossings only (not on cruises or round-the-world voyages).

What will you need if you want to travel with your pet on an airplane?

Your dog will probably be required to travel in the cargo section of the plane, and he must be placed in a regulation kennel, which you can buy or rent from a neighborhood store or purchase from the airline. It *must* be sturdy (so it will not buckle if something falls on it), have a security lock, contain ventilation holes on the sides, and have a leakproof bottom. Your pet should be able to stand in it without hitting the top of the case, turn around with ease, and lie down comfortably. The kennel should have a water dish inside and, attached to the outside, a bag containing canned food and a can opener.

A Toy or very tiny pet might be allowed to accompany you in the passenger compartment, provided he is in a box that conforms to proper standards in case he must be placed elsewhere. Keep your pet under your seat when the "fasten seatbelt" sign is flashed, and don't allow him to run about during the flight.

Some airlines will allow only one dog to travel in the passenger compartment, and he and his owner will occupy a seat called the bulkhead. Check in early or call ahead to receive this priority and, again, have your pet's kennel with you if the airline decides he must travel in the cargo compartment.

Many airlines issue pamphlets stating traveling requirements and care and feeding information. Identification forms are provided and copies are attached to the kennel and to the collar of the dog.

When making reservations, insist that "TRAVELING WITH DOG" is marked on your ticket so that all personnel know that you and the dog belong together. Select the most direct route to your destination, avoiding transfers to other planes and stopovers. If the journey is split among different airlines, make sure the booking agent has your pet's passage confirmed on all of them. Your dog's fare is determined according to his weight and the weight of his container.

Can you fly your dog home ahead of the family?

It is not advisable to fly an unaccompanied dog to any land other than the United States. In the States, you can feel confident that as long as your pet and his crate are properly tagged, he will be safe if his destination is New York, for The Animalport at Kennedy International Airport (Jamaica, New York, 11430, U.S.A.) will board your pet at the facility until you pick him up. The Animalport is run by the ASPCA (American Society for the Prevention of Cruelty to Animals) and is the first shelter of its kind in the Western hemisphere. It is devoted exclusively to animal air travelers and is open twenty-four hours a day, seven days a week, so you can retrieve your pet at any time.

Whether your pet travels alone or accompanied, he must have valid papers and will most likely undergo a brief physical examination before being released in your care.

Can you take your pet on a train?

Short-run and commuter lines will usually overlook the presence of an animal in his carrying case, although there is always a chance that someone might complain. On long-distance travel, the animal, again, in his carrying case, can be deposited in the baggage compartment, and you can visit him en route. If there is no baggage area, he might not be permitted to travel with you, so check with the train line ahead of time. When you travel by train, you are totally responsible for your pet's feeding and care.

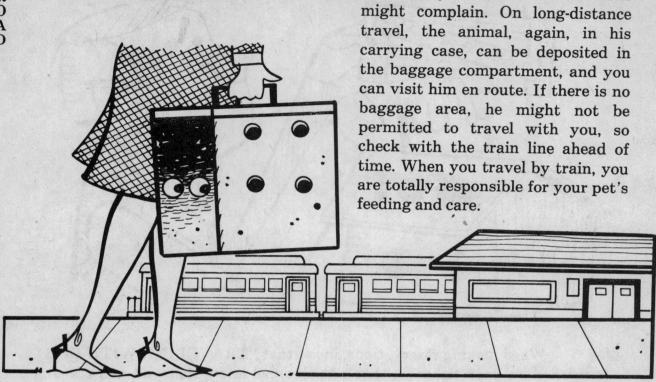

Is bus transportation a good travel alternative for your pet?

Transportation of dogs by bus is prohibited by the Interstate Commerce Commission. Therefore, long-distance lines cannot permit a dog aboard. Local buses will usually raise no objection if your pet is in a suitable container and does not disturb anyone. (In many European countries, dogs trot on and off buses beside their owners, riding free of charge or receiving a special dog ticket.)

146

Where should a dog sit when he rides in a car?

The best place for the dog is on the floor in the back. Then, if the brakes are applied abruptly, he won't be hurled forward, injuring himself on the dashboard or any other protruding object. Don't allow your dog near the steering wheel, and make sure he doesn't leap around the car or hang his paws over the front seat, distracting the driver.

Will car travel disturb your dog?

Take your pet on some short car trips. If he appears unaffected, special precautions for longer trips probably won't be necessary. However, if on a long journey he starts to swallow hard and drool, pull off the highway immediately and walk him in the fresh air for about thirty minutes.

If you know your pet becomes car sick, buy a preventative over-the-counter drug. (The amount given depends on his weight, so read the instructions carefully. The drug is usually administered one hour before travel.) Serve your dog a light meal prior to departure and give him snacks every three hours during the ride.

Should you allow your dog to hang his head out of the car window?

No, for a great many reasons. Your dog may decide to leap out the window to chase something; the rush of air can inflame his sinuses and lead to ear problems; insects and dust can flit into his eyes, causing serious irritation or impairment of sight; a lit cigarette thrown from the car ahead can fly into his mouth; he will probably be breathing poisonous fumes from the highway traffic. In addition, another animal or automobile may approach to greet him, possibly resulting in a car accident, injury, and perhaps even death.

Can you leave the dog in the car if you park in the shade?

The car that was in the shade when you left may be in the blazing sun by the time you return. If you must leave him, roll all the windows down at least 2 inches and check on him every half hour. A dog can contract heat prostration even while you are with him if the sun is beating down on the car. If your pet appears distraught, soak a cloth in ice-cold water, wring it out, and wipe him down. Then soak and wring out the cloth again and force your pet to lie on it. Resume traveling at a cooler time of day.

Should you transport your dog in the trunk of your car?

No. The dog may die from inhaling carbon monoxide fumes or he may suffocate. He may be overcome by heat when the sun beats down on the trunk or freeze to death in the winter. He can also incur serious bruises and lacerations from bumping around in the trunk. If you stuff your pet in the trunk because he bothers you when you drive, purchase a cage or barrier especially constructed for transporting dogs in cars.

What is the easiest way to travel with several dogs?

There are grilles available that prevent animals from leaving the rear section of the car or sturdy cages in which each dog may be transported separately. The cages are particularly beneficial in case of accident. They will not buckle under impact, preventing the occupant from being crushed to death.

Should you honk your horn when a stray runs across traffic?

Blowing your horn will terrify and confuse the dog. Gradually, slow your vehicle, forcing those behind you to do the same. This will give the animal a chance to reach his destination. Do not pick up the pet, claiming him as your own, even though he is not wearing a collar unless you report it to the police and/or the animal control center in the area. If he does belong to someone who is searching for him, at least his whereabouts will be known.

149

Wouldn't it be dangerous to stop if you hit a dog on the highway?

If a dog shoots out in front of a motorist, it is frequently impossible to halt instantly. Sometimes, however, it is possible to slow down or move to the shoulder of the road. If you do hit a dog, try to find someplace to stop and walk back to ascertain if anything can be done for the animal. Then, report the accident to police in the vicinity in which the accident occurred.

You saw an accident in which a driver hit and killed a dog and never stopped. What should you have done?

When you witness a hit-and-run accident, jot down the license number of the car, its make and color, and any identifying marks (such as the dealer's name and address). Then report the incident to the police. With the information you supply, they can obtain the name of the offender by checking the central files of the Motor Vehicle Bureau. In addition, they will have the information available if the owner makes inquiries about his dog.

Who is responsible for paying the medical expenses if you take an injured dog to a hospital?

The person who takes the animal to the hospital is responsible for the medical fees if the pet's owner cannot be located or refuses to pay the bill.

If you hit a dog, can the owner sue you?

Because the important point is that the dog should receive medical attention as quickly as possible, it is good to know that the driver of an automobile is rarely in a position to be sued for hitting or killing a dog who is on the road. The law says almost everywhere that "a dog must be leashed and under the control of his owner at all times." But in some states, failure to report the accident will make you guilty of a misdemeanor and classify you as a hit-and-run driver.

While driving, you come upon an injured animal. What should you do?

Most accidents involving pets occur directly in front of their own homes (rather than miles away as many imagine), so try to find help from nearby residents who might know or own the dog. Remember, a pet that is lying down is not necessarily a hopeless case. He may be suffering from internal bleeding that will not prove fatal if treated in time. Check his condition and, if possible, help him. Otherwise, he may be hit again and again, and ultimately killed.

Medical Care

- **First Aid**
- **Treating Injured Dogs**
- **Selecting a Veterinarian**
- **Symptoms of Illness**
- **Internal Injuries**
- **Taking Your Dog's Temperature**
- **Taking Your Dog's Pulse**
- **Administering Liquid Medication**
- **Swallowing Pills**
- **Eye Disorders**
- **Ear Care**
- **Respiratory Ailments**
- **Dental Care**
- **Shock**
- **Burns**
- **Bleeding**

- **Splinters**
- **Electric Shock**
- **The "Bloat"**
- **Poison**
- **Bee and Wasp Stings**
- **Hip Dysplasia**
- **Rabies**
- **Distemper**
- **Hepatitis**
- **Leptospirosis**
- **Immunization**
- **Ringworm**
- **Mange**
- **Eczema**
- **Hospital Care**

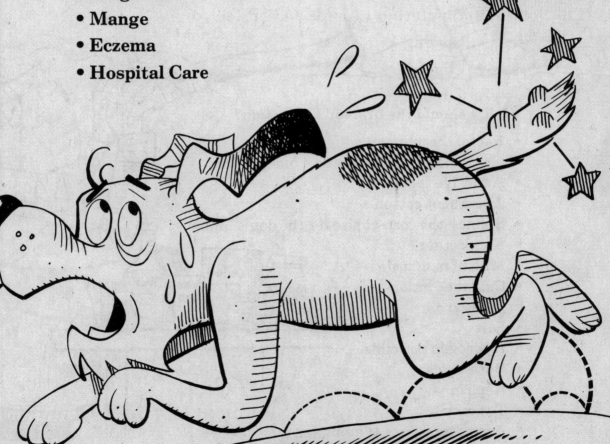

Is it necessary to learn first aid?

Immediate medical attention eases a pet's suffering and, in some instances, means the difference between life and death. However, remember that first aid is treatment given to an injured animal *before* regular medical aid can be obtained. It is not intended to replace professional care.

Practice first aid, so when the time comes to use it, you will be confident. During thirty-minute sessions, show your dog the contents of the first-aid kit and say, "Now I'm going to give Pete first aid." Begin practice with bandaging. Always use the same words before you start, and laugh and talk to your dog while practicing. This will make him easier to handle if an emergency really occurs, and you will know exactly what to do.

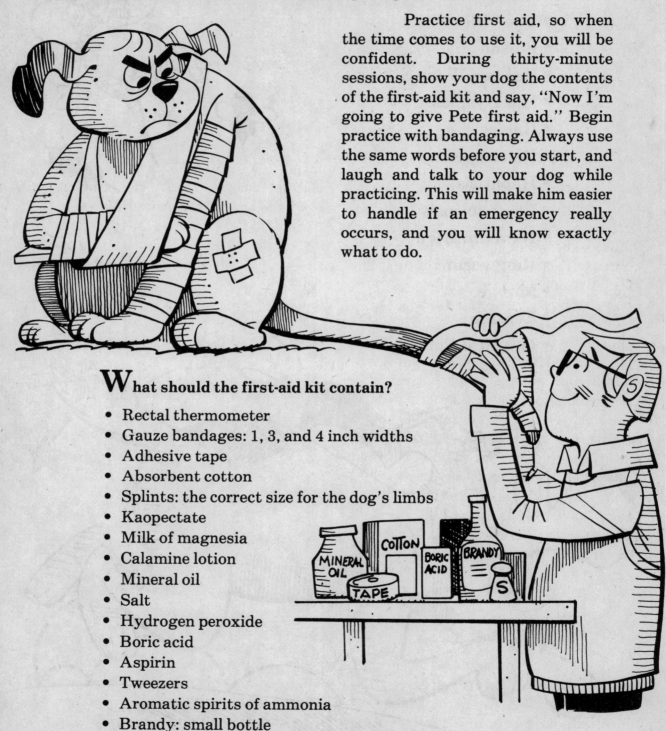

What should the first-aid kit contain?

- Rectal thermometer
- Gauze bandages: 1, 3, and 4 inch widths
- Adhesive tape
- Absorbent cotton
- Splints: the correct size for the dog's limbs
- Kaopectate
- Milk of magnesia
- Calamine lotion
- Mineral oil
- Salt
- Hydrogen peroxide
- Boric acid
- Aspirin
- Tweezers
- Aromatic spirits of ammonia
- Brandy: small bottle

You should have two first-aid kits: one in the home and one in the car.

How should you approach an injured animal?

Be cautious when you near an animal—even your own—who has been hurt. He will probably be terrified and unnerved and may think that you were the cause of his misfortune. So keep your face away from his mouth, safe from biting distance. If he doesn't look as if he is going to attack you, move the back of your hand, fingers curled under, slowly toward him. Call the dog by name (if you know it) and speak softly, using words he might understand, perhaps "good dog." Avoid holding anything in your hand that might frighten him and don't move too quickly. If he accepts your advances, it will be easier to treat him.

Is it possible to prevent an injured dog from biting you?

Before treating a pet's wounds, it is best to tie his mouth closed so he will not bite you if you happen to touch a painful spot. Make a muzzle from gauze, a belt, a necktie, or any item that is long and flat. Before you apply the muzzle, however, check that the dog's mouth and nose are free of blood or mucus. Do not tie the muzzle too tightly, hindering the dog's breathing. To make the muzzle, tie a loose knot in the center of your chosen material so that there is a large loop. Hold the ends, one in each hand, and slide the loop over the pet's nose to a point as close to his eyes as possible. Now pull the ends, tightening the loop around the nose so that the dog cannot open his mouth. Bring the ends under the chin and make a knot there, then take the ends, one on each side of the face, under the ears, and tie them together at the back of his head.

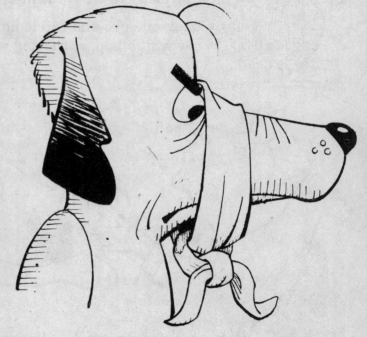

Can you tell when a dog has suffered internal injuries?

Check his gums. White gums are a sign of internal bleeding. However, even if you are not sure but have good reason to believe his internal organs are injured, bind his stomach and chest with 4-inch-wide bandages. If you don't have bandages, rip any available material to make the strips. This will keep his organs in position until a vet sees him. He should be brought to a vet immediately.

How do you remove an injured dog from the road?

Although you shouldn't move an animal who has been hit by a car, sometimes he has to be taken off a busy road. First, ease a blanket, to be used as a stretcher, under him. Don't put your face in biting distance, and, if possible, cover your hands and arms. He may bite them to register disapproval if you touch a painful spot. Place the animal on the side of the road where oncoming traffic can see him. If you need help, his body will attract attention and someone might stop.

Is there any way to tell if the injured dog is still alive?

Gently open one eye and tap it lightly with your index finger. If the dog is alive, the eye will roll up, or the dog will blink. If there is no reaction, the dog is dead.

What is a dog's normal body temperature?

Regular body heat is usually 101.5°F. in medium and large dogs, and 102°F. in Toy breeds. To check your dog's temperature, smear a rectal thermometer with mineral oil. Roll the pet on his side and gently insert the instrument into his rectum as far as it will go without a great deal of pressure. Place one hand on your pet's body to prevent him from making a sudden move or running off. Remove the thermometer after five minutes. If the temperature varies from the norm by one degree, up or down, the dog is sick. If it's higher or lower than the norm by more than one degree, your pet is very ill.

How do you take a dog's pulse?

The pet's pulse can be felt on his chest, near the second joint in his foreleg. Simply place four fingers beside the bone and gently move them. Then pause. Move them again and pause. Your middle finger will suddenly detect the beat, beat, beat you are looking for. Small dogs have a high pulse rate of 120 to 150 beats per minute. Larger breeds range from 90 to 120 beats per minute. Practice taking your pet's pulse. If an emergency arises, you will know exactly where to find it, and you will be familiar with his regular pulse rate.

Will your pet resist taking liquid medication?

Your pet, like all others, will resist, so try mixing the medication into his food. If he isn't fooled, a more direct method will be necessary. The medication usually comes in a small vial. Hold it in your left hand while pulling out the side of your dog's mouth with your right hand, making a triangular pocket. Pour the prescribed amount into this pocket, then quickly let go and hold your pet's mouth shut. Help him to swallow by tilting his head backward *just a little bit* and/or rubbing his throat.

How can you make your dog swallow a pill?

Dogs have a great ability to keep pills hidden in their cheeks. So smother the pill with something tasty, or make it slippery with butter or margarine. Then, with your left hand, take hold of the dog's lower jaw and press his lips against his teeth. This will force him to open his mouth. When he opens up, use one finger of your right hand to push the pill toward the back of his tongue. Then close and hold his mouth shut. Tilt his head backward very *slightly* and caress his throat until you feel him swallowing. If the animal appears to be choking, release his mouth. A pill can accidentally go down his windpipe and kill him within seconds.

Can you tell when a dog is in shock?

After an accident, a dog is often in shock. Your ability to recognize shock and to act quickly is the greatest assistance you can provide. His eyes will be glassy; his breathing, rapid and shallow; his gums, pale. He often loses the contents of his bladder and bowels. The pet will not necessarily be lying down. He might be running around in a crazy fashion. His temperature will be below normal, but if these other signs appear, you need not confirm this. Wrap

him in something warm immediately and rush him to the hospital, where he will receive intravenous fluid, blood, and any other necessary treatment. If professional help is not available, position the dog's head slightly lower than his body. Add sugar to warm water or milk and give it to him. If his breathing remains faint, have him drink some black coffee or brandy in warm water in the same way you administer liquid medication when he refuses to swallow. If he simply can't swallow, give him two or three (no more) quick whiffs of aromatic spirits of ammonia.

What should you do if your pet is burned?

If it is a minor fire or hot-water burn, apply a cold, wet tea bag or compress to the burned area. It will remove the heat sensation. Repeat this several times. Then apply oil or ointment in generous amounts to keep the skin supple. Dress the wound with a clean bandage or pad kept in place with adhesive tape. The bandages must be changed twice daily. The pet may permanently lose his fur, so even if the spot does not become infected, it is advisable to consult a veterinarian to see what can be done.

If the burn is extensive, do not treat it yourself. Take the dog to the vet immediately.

If the dog suffers a chemical burn, an alkaline solution must be applied (1 pint of warm water and 1 tablespoon of baking soda), or wash the area with milk of magnesia.

Why does the dog constantly rub his face and shake his head?

He has something caught in his mouth or throat. Under a strong light, open his mouth wide. If you can see and grasp the object, gently pull it out. If you can see it but cannot reach it, or cannot see it but the dog keeps rubbing and shaking, take him to the veterinarian.

How good is a dog's eyesight?

His vision is not as sharp as yours. He sees everything in various shades of grey, and he is near-sighted. That is why he jumps up on people to greet them: he is eager to get a better look. His eyeball is like yours, but it is embedded within a bony structure for protective purposes and has three lids, two of which have split-second reflexes to further protect the lens.

Why does your pet paw at his eyes?

If your pet has been running in the sand, hanging his head out of a car window, or chasing about in the underbrush, he may paw his eyes because they are irritated. Use human eyedrops in a short plastic dropper (a long glass stopper may injure your dog's eyes if he moves) to relieve the irritation. If there is something in his eye, try to remove it with the corner of a clean cloth. Never use anything sharp because, if the dog gives a sudden jerk to get away, the object could enter his eye and blind him. If he still paws after three days of eyedrops, take the dog to the vet.

Is there anything wrong with a dog whose eyelids turn in?

Inturned eyelids are a sign that your dog has been excessively inbred. And although the condition can be corrected, he is almost certain to have other defects as well. Other occular signs of too much inbreeding are eyelids that turn out or an extra row of eyelashes.

The dog paws at his eyes, smothers his head in his paws, and squints continuously as if it is difficult for him to stay awake. Is he really tired?

The dog is in extreme pain, either from a serious eye disorder or a terrible headache. Take him to the vet as soon as possible.

Will the dog rip off his bandages after an eye operation?

Once, it was impossible to perform certain types of eye surgery because the dog would tear off the bandages and scratch and rip the stitches, interrupting the healing process. Today, soft contact lenses are used to protect the eyes after surgery. They are very soothing, so the dog rarely tries to dislodge them.

How can you tell if your dog is becoming blind?

Place your index finger about 4 inches in front of your pet's eyes. Gradually, move your finger to the right, about 36 inches, then to the left, then up and down. If your dog follows with his eyes, moving his head as required, his eyesight so far is normal. Next, have someone hold the dog on a leash while you walk away. Move 10 feet away, then 20 feet, 30 feet, and 60 feet. Call his name from each distance and tell your friend to drop the leash. If the dog runs toward you in a straight line, he's fine. If he goes off to either side, hesitates on the way, or looks confused, his sight is not as good as it used to be. (You can also move furniture into unaccustomed positions to see if he bumps into it or appears to have difficulty avoiding it.) If it is obvious that his eyesight is defective, stop the test because your dog may become upset, and take him to the vet for a complete eye examination.

What do you do for a dog with red and inflamed eyes?

Use human eyedrops with a short plastic stopper. The inflammation will probably clear within three days. If it doesn't, see a veterinarian.

Are particular breeds subject to eye defects?

When you buy your dog, go to a breeder with a good reputation and inspect the eyes of the dam closely (and the sire too, if possible). About 40% of serious eye defects are inherited. Although you should not avoid a particular breed because it is subject to certain diseases, be alert when buying, and on the lookout as the dog grows older. Breeds that are sometimes prone to eye disorders are Basenjis, Basset Hounds, Bedlington Terriers, Bloodhounds, Cocker Spaniels, Collies, Irish Setters, Labrador Retrievers, Norwegian Elkhounds, Poodles, Schnauzers (miniatures), Sealyhams, and St. Bernards.

Are cataracts inherited?

Yes. But some come about through old age, drug therapy, or trauma. In any event, the dog usually does not lose his sight completely, and if taken into strange surroundings, he can cope when accompanied by a human companion. The disease becomes noticeable when the eye turns pale blue and ceases to glisten. Today, cataracts can be removed, and these operations are nearly always successful.

Which ailments are usually hereditary?

Common inherited ailments:

• *Hip dysplasia,* a malformation of the bone and socket—and a variety of other malformations of the legs and hips.

• *Intervertebral disluxation,* a spine disease often observed in Dachshunds.

• *Diarrhea,* prevalent in German Shepherds and Boxers.

• *Progressive retinal atrophy* or *retinal detachment,* often causing blindness in Collies and Bedlingtons.

• *Inturned or out-turned eyelids,* which cause severe eye discomfort.

• *Epilepsy,* noticeable when the dog experiences many fits.

• *Glaucoma,* often resulting in blindness.

• *Diabetes.*

• *Tetany,* a physiologic mineral imbalance exhibited in Highland Terriers when they have muscle spasms.

Dogs with any of these defects should not be bred.

Your dog's nose drips. Is anything wrong?

If he doesn't have a cough and generally appears healthy, he might have an allergy. Allergies become apparent when the dog is about two years of age or older. Grass, shrubs, leaves, ragweed, dandelions, goldenrod, and other growing things might be the cause, as well as household dust, feathers, or rugs. Wirehaired Terriers seem particularly prone to allergies.

When your dog is out in the sun, he develops a skin eruption a few days later. Why?

Your dog is allergic to the sun, so try to keep him in the shade as much as possible. Soothe the erupted skin with calamine lotion, which will stop the itching and, in turn, prevent the dog from scratching and inflaming the area. Collies, Shetland Sheepdogs, German Shepherds, and dogs with white, lightly-colored, or mottled nostrils are often affected by the sun.

Does the environment affect a dog's nose and lungs?

The most important study on this matter was conducted by the University of Pennsylvania School of Veterinary Medicine in 1965. It concluded that canines under five years of age did not suffer any ill effects from pollutants. After that age, however, the breathing of bad air caused coughing, wheezing, and hyperventilating, and the dogs contracted influenza, pleurisy, emphysema, sinusitis, and cancer.

Does cigarette smoke affect the dog's health?

Passive inhalation of smoke is dangerous. Your dog could develop cancer from cigarette smoke.

If your dog sleeps in the garage, will the air there make him ill?

The fumes from the car, which contain carbon monoxide, can give your dog lung cancer if he breathes them continuously.

Why does your dog paw his nose and rub it against the floor?

Examine his nose. He may be troubled by a hair caught in his nostril. However, if you cannot see anything, take him to the vet. Your dog might have a malignant tumor growing inside the nasal cavity.

Your dog's nose has been running for a while, and now he has a hacking cough. What's wrong with him?

He may have bronchitis, which must be treated by a vet. The next time your dog starts to sniffle, treat him as you would a member of the family who has a cold: Keep him away from drafts, see that he gets plenty of rest, and give him aspirin. This will help prevent the development of a severe illness.

Can dogs contract tuberculosis?

Dogs, including strays, are very resistant to tuberculosis, even when they eat birds who have the disease. Short-nosed breeds are more susceptible than long-nosed breeds, but, again, the disease is very rare in canines today.

How do you treat a nosebleed?

Keep the dog still and apply a cold, damp cloth to the nose and the area surrounding it. If the bleeding occurs on a regular basis, have the veterinarian check for growths inside the dog's nasal cavity.

Are Collies more susceptible to nasal cancer than any other breed?

Unfortunately, yes. They have an inherited tendency for nose disorders. However, there are thousands of Collies who will never be affected, so if you are considering purchasing a Collie, do not let this sway your decision.

There is nothing wrong with hitting a dog on the nose to correct unwanted behavior. True or False?

Although some obedience trainers recommend the practice, striking the pet's nose causes him intense pain. The thousands of nerve endings at the tip of his nose, which transmit this excruciating pain, may become permanently damaged. Also, the many small bones supporting the nasal cavity can be very easily broken or knocked out of position. *Never* hit your dog on his nose. If you must hit him, his rump is better padded for the blow.

How can you rid your dog's ears of wax?

Warm some mineral oil in the palm of your hand, then with a teaspoon, place a few drops into the ear, holding the dog's head so that the oil runs in. After a few minutes, rub the ear very gently from the outside. Then *gently* insert a cotton swab (do not push too deeply) and wipe out any accumulation you can reach. Later, clean the other ear.

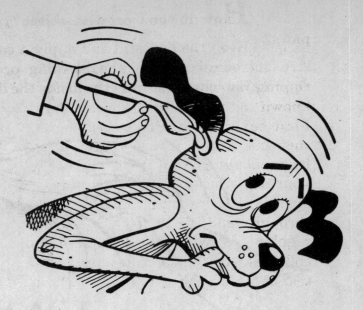

How can you stop the bleeding of an injured ear or paw?

If the bleeding is caused by a superficial scratch or cut, make sure the wound is free of glass or splinters. Then, simply wash the cut with cold water, apply a disinfectant that is not harmful if swallowed, and after the disinfectant has soaked into the cut, let the dog go on his way. He will probably spend a great deal of time licking the wound, and this is natural.

If the bleeding is severe, place a clean pad over the wound and press it down with your thumb (or your entire hand if it is a large wound). When the flow of blood stops, apply disinfectant and bandage the wound, covering the bandage with wide adhesive tape so it cannot be pulled off easily.

Profuse bleeding must be stopped immediately. If pressure applied to the wound does not stop the bleeding, a tourniquet must be used. If an artery has been injured—*bright red blood spurting from the wound*—then apply the tourniquet between the wound and the heart. If a vein has been injured—*dark red blood flowing evenly from the wound*—apply the tourniquet on the side of the wound farthest from the heart. (Bright red blood that oozes slowly from the wound is from a shallow or flesh wound and is usually not serious.) Release the pressure on the tourniquet every fifteen minutes to allow the normal flow of blood to other parts of the body. If the bleeding does not stop within a short time, professional aid is essential and might even be a matter of life and death.

How do you prevent a dog from ripping his bandages from his paws?

To prevent your dog from ripping his bandages, make what is known as an Elizabethan collar. First cut a circle out of cardboard, then cut a hole in the center just large enough so that it will slip over your dog's head. Now, punch a few holes in the cardboard, thread string through, and tie it to the dog's regular collar. The Elizabethan collar should hinder his ability to tear at his bandages.

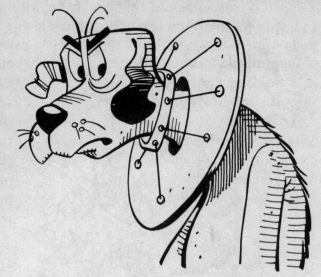

Why does your dog shake his head violently?

He probably has ear mites. You might also find, upon examination, that his ear flaps are swollen. Take the dog to the vet as soon as possible. But in the meantime, cover his ears with a nylon stocking to prevent them from tossing when he shakes his head and to keep him from scratching and infecting the area further. (The vet may tell you that the dog has a hematoma as a result of the infection and, if this is so, blood will have to be drained until the swelling goes down. But if the ear mites have not been present very long, only a thorough cleaning will be necessary.)

What is the best way to remove a splinter, thorn, or piece of glass from the dog's paw?

Position the dog under a bright light and pull out the offending object with a pair of tweezers, removing it at the *same angle* in which it penetrated so a piece doesn't break off and remain imbedded. Although the paw pad is fairly tough, the flesh between the toes and the toes themselves are extremely sensitive, so be careful not to hurt your animal. Otherwise, he might snap at you. It is advisable to muzzle your dog before you attempt to remove the object.

Why is the dog walking strangely?

First, check his claws. If they are too long, they might be causing him to apply pressure on the wrong muscles or bones. If this is so, soak your dog's paws in warm water, then coat his claws with mineral oil and trim them. Also check his toes. If tar, snow, or rock salt is stuck between them, pressing on extremely delicate tissue, he will also walk peculiarly. If this is the case, clip the hair from between his toes, then massage his pads, toes, and the areas in between with mineral oil.

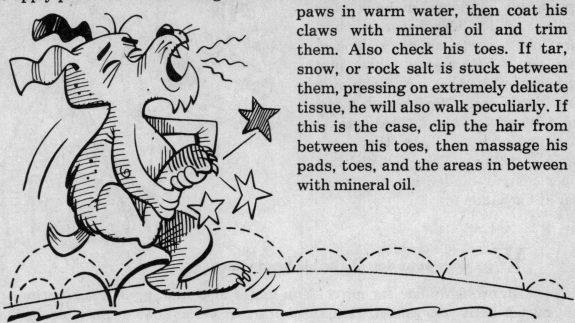

Why can't you always treat your pet yourself? Why do you have to take him to the vet?

The diagnosis you make may not be correct. A veterinarian with many years of medical study can diagnose symptoms quickly and correctly, and he can prescribe drugs that are not obtainable over the counter. It is fine to treat your dog for minor injuries and illnesses. But if the complaint does not improve or becomes worse, the vet is the person to consult for the sake of your pet's well being.

Which symptoms are forerunners of illness?

A rise or drop in temperature and an increase or decrease in pulse rate are signs of illness, particularly if they occur with one or more of the following:

- Lack of vitality
- Change of posture with tail hanging down
- Excessive apathy or sleepiness
- Continuous activity with little or no rest or sleep
- Vomiting: more than once
- Diarrhea: over twelve hours
- Blood in stool
- Constipation
- Blood in urine
- Deep orange urine
- Excessive thirst
- Loss of appetite for over twenty-four hours
- Noticeable reduction in weight
- Coughing
- Sneezing
- Inflamed eyes
- Eyes discharging and dull
- Dry or running nose
- Coated tongue
- Continuous scratching
- A healthy coat turned rough and lusterless
- Dragging hindquarters along the floor

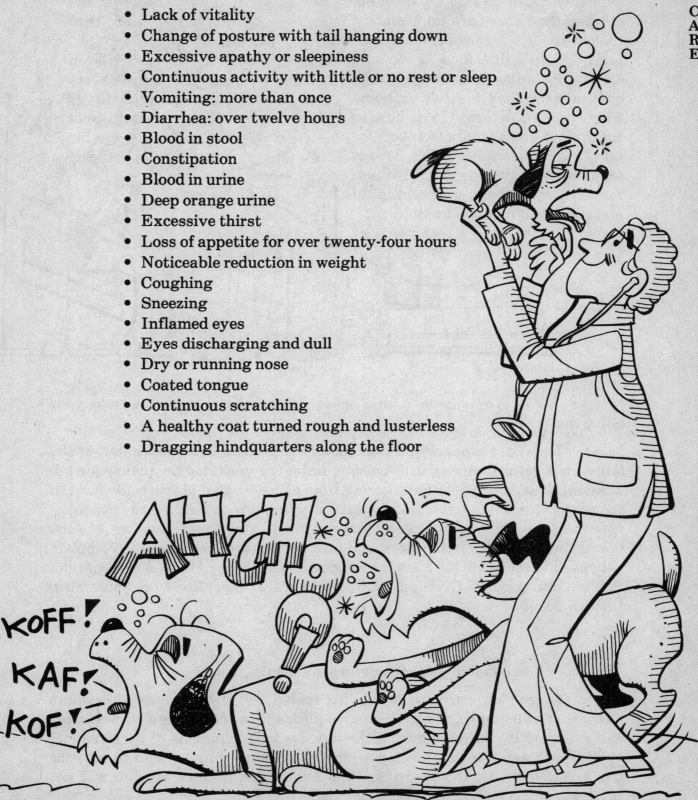

Should a sick or injured dog be placed in a hospital?

If the recovery period is going to be long, the dog should be placed in a hospital. After surgery, the pet may require intravenous feedings or blood transfusions, or he may rip open his stitches, and these are immediately tended to in a well-supervised hospital. If a dog breaks a bone, it is easier to confine him in a strange environment than in his own home where he is accustomed to rushing to the door to greet family members, or hurrying to the window when he sees the neighbor's cat passing. Visit him regularly when he is in the hospital and exercise him if it is feasible.

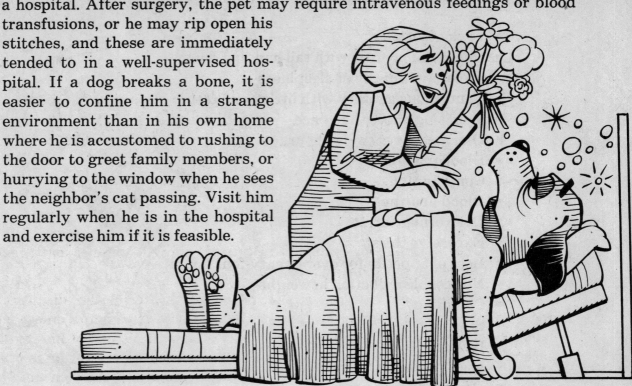

Will a university with a school of veterinary medicine treat your ailing dog?

He would probably be treated very well there with the benefit of the latest medical techniques. However, in order for your dog to qualify for admission, he usually has to be suffering from a disease that is especially hard to conquer. If your dog falls into this category, inquire at your nearby school of veterinary medicine before taking him elsewhere. There are about twenty such institutions in the United States, and medical fees are reasonable. A complete list of schools is available from the American Veterinary Medical Association, Public Information Division, 930 North Meacham Road, Schaumburg, Illinois, 60196.

What should you consider when selecting a vet?

Obtain an estimate of his fee scale. Ask if he makes after-hours emergency calls for regular patients. Inquire about office hours on weekends and evenings if you work during the day. Seek the opinions of other animal owners who use this vet. Once you find a vet, allow him to tend to all your dog's health needs. If you dodge from one doctor to another, you will not receive as much interest or cooperation from them.

Your pet has a serious illness which might require emergency treatment at any time. What should you do?

Establish your dog as a regular patient of a veterinarian, discuss the dog's condition with the doctor, and ask if he makes after-hours emergency calls. A vet will usually answer these calls if the animal is one of his regular patients. If a vet first meets the dog on an emergency, he will not be familiar with the dog's medical history (he might not even come to treat your animal). If you move, establish your dog with a new vet, even if he just had a check-up, so you will be prepared in the event of an emergency.

What are the symptoms of heartworm?

The symptoms are extreme weakness, heavy breathing, noticeable weight loss, and coughing. Unfortunately, once these signs appear, the worms will have been in your dog's body for about six months, and he will already be seriously ill. Mosquitoes carry the larvae of these thin, white worms. When the mosquitoes feed on the dog, the larvae are released into the dog's tissues and eventually nest in his heart. There, they mature to their full length (about 5 to 15 inches) and block the blood flow, damaging not only the heart but the kidneys and liver as well. Keep your pet away from swarms of mosquitoes, don't let him stay outdoors too long when they are flying about, and bring the dog to the vet every spring to test for this deadly disease.

Can you cure your dog of heartworm?

There is no do-it-yourself remedy. Treatment must be administered by a veterinarian. It consists of a number of intravenous injections of an arsenic compound to kill the mature worms, and the amount of medication must be carefully monitored so it does not kill the dog. Another drug follows the injections. This destroys unhatched larvae. When the worms and larvae die, they break into bits and are carried away in the dog's bloodstream. The dog must be kept still because exertion increases blood flow, and in turn, dead worms may lodge in vital blood vessels. In extremely serious cases and when all other methods fail, the worms are pulled out of the heart with tweezers. Because there is no preventive vaccine for heartworm, the best course is to take precautionary action.

Should you give your dog over-the-counter medication that cures worms without seeing a vet?

No. You do not know what type of worms are present, and each type has to be eliminated in a different manner. If over-the-counter medication is not given properly, it can kill your dog along with the worms. So, if you think your dog is infected, take your pet's stool sample to the vet. After examining the stool, he will be able to prescribe the proper medication.

Your dog is well fed at home, but he still raids garbage cans. Will eating trash make him sick?

It may poison him or give him "the bloat." If he contracts food poisoning, induce vomiting by placing 2 teaspoons of salt on the back of his

tongue. When the vomiting stops, feed him some egg white. The bloat is caused when he eats strange combinations of food that do not agree with one another or are slightly spoiled. You can see his stomach actually blow up, and although it sometimes goes down just as quickly as it rises, he can die almost immediately. So, keep your pet away from the garbage.

Your dog chews on electric cords. What should you do if he gets electrocuted?

Prevention is better than cure. Try to keep all electric cords out of his reach. If possible, fasten the wires to the wall. However, should your pet meet with a mishap, *REMOVE THE ELECTRICAL PLUG FROM THE OUTLET BEFORE YOU TOUCH THE DOG.* Otherwise, the volts may pass through your body too, especially if the pet has urinated from fright and you are standing in the puddle. Usually, the pet becomes completely rigid and leaps into the air before falling into a heap on the floor. Once you've disconnected the cord, jerk it out of the animal's mouth and apply artificial respiration. If he revives, give him strong black coffee or brandy in water to stimulate his heartbeat.

Is there any other way to induce vomiting if a dog swallows something he shouldn't have?

Mix peroxide and water together in equal parts. Use 1 teaspoonful for every 5 pounds of your dog's weight. Get it down his throat as quickly as possible, using the same method for administering liquid medication.

How should a dog be treated if he swallows poison?

Make him vomit as quickly as possible. Look on the package of the substance he has swallowed for information about an antidote and, if possible, give it to him. Then rush him to the veterinarian. If there is no doctor available, give the dog an enema.

What should you do for a dog who has swallowed a sleeping pill or tranquilizer?

If he swallowed only one pill and he is a medium-size or large dog, do nothing. If he is a Toy or small breed, make him vomit, give him black coffee, and do everything you can to keep him moving and awake. Do the same for a dog of any size who has gobbled many pills, but in addition, bring him to the vet as soon as possible.

Will it harm your pet if you spray your plants with insecticides?

Read the instructions very carefully before you use such agents. If the label states that the chemical is poisonous to dogs, it might be better to have a dead plant than a dead dog.

If a wasp or bee stings your dog, what should you do?

Mix baking soda and water to make a thick paste and apply it to the sting. If your pet shows signs of breathlessness and he seems to be in great pain, rush him to the vet. He may be allergic to the sting, and an antihistamine injection will be necessary to counteract the poison.

If your dog swallows antifreeze, what should you do?

Dogs seem to think antifreeze is a treat and will go after it again and again, even though it makes them sick. Usually, they vomit almost immediately after lapping it up. But don't take any chances. Administer the medication that is used in cases of poisoning.

Your dog likes to jump out of car windows, house windows, and anything else that seems worth a leap. Can he injure himself?

Close your windows, especially if anything occurs that is likely to frighten your dog. If he jumps from a window, he may break a bone, which can only be treated by a vet. (If a bone is broken, the dog must be moved on a stretcher.) If he doesn't break anything, calm him down after the fall by talking gently and stroking him.

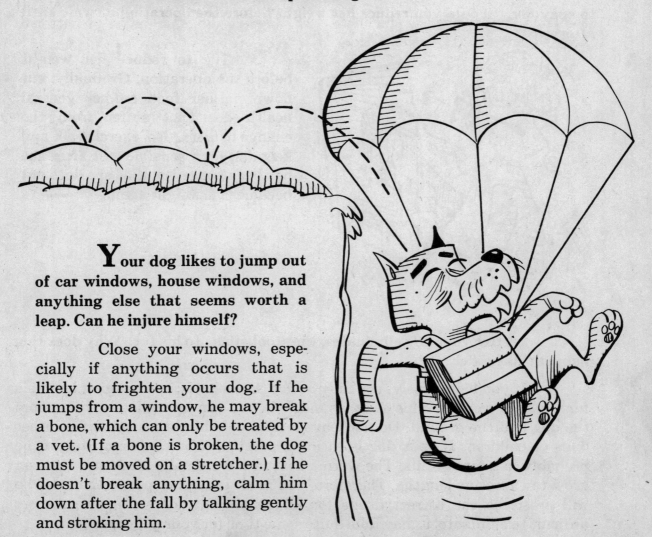

Your dog likes coffee? Should you allow him to drink it?

The caffeine might give your dog heart palpitations. If he must drink coffee on a regular basis, make it decaffeinated.

Your overweight female has already had two litters, and you want to spay her. Should you reduce her weight before the operation or wait until afterward?

Try to reduce her weight before the operation. Gradually, cut down on her food so her general health does not suffer from the change in diet. Also, exercise her and keep her on a sensible diet after she has been spayed so that she does not become overweight again.

After your dog eliminates, the stool sticks to his fur. Why does this happen? Is he sick?

If you look closely, you may notice that whatever is hanging upon his fur is alive—worms. Wipe away as much as you can immediately, both from the dog and the ground. Do not leave anything behind that can infect other dogs or children. If your dog is eating a great deal but is losing weight, he probably has tapeworms. The worms nest in the animal's intestines and can grow to excessive lengths. Therefore, you must take your pet to the vet who will prescribe the correct drugs for killing the intruders. Tapeworms are difficult to eliminate; it may take quite some time for your pet to recover.

Your dog flops down on his front legs, leaving his hindquarters up in the air, and sometimes whimpers. Is something wrong?

He probably has a stomach ache or an intestinal disorder. Check his stool for blood, worms, or mucus. If any of these are found, your pet needs immediate medical treatment. If these signs are absent and he continues this strange behavior, take him and a stool sample to the vet for analysis.

At what age can a dog be diagnosed for hip dysplasia?

Hip dysplasia is an inherited malformation of the hip socket and the leg bone that should fit into it. The condition is aggravated if a young puppy becomes overweight or races about too much. Hip dysplasia is found more often in larger breeds or animals weighing over 35 pounds. If you want to mate your dog at an early age, he (she) can be X-rayed for the defect after he is twelve weeks old, but if there is no cause for haste, it is advisable to wait until the animal is one year old, when a definite diagnosis can be made. *Under no circumstances should a canine with hip dysplasia be bred.* Otherwise, this serious defect will be passed on from generation to generation.

Why is there so much fuss about rabies?

A friend from Hungary related that forty years ago when a dog who was suspected of having rabies bit someone, the town crier would go from house to house warning mothers and children to stay indoors, church bells would be rung, and men would go out with pitchforks to capture and kill the rabid dog. Every now and then, someone would peek from behind a curtain or crack open the door to make sure the mad dog was not around before he ventured outside.

The rabies virus attacks the nervous system and results in death. If a rabid dog bites someone, the victim nearly always dies too. So it is extremely important that your dog receive immunization. Since squirrels and wolves

sometimes carry rabies, which is transferred when one animal licks the saliva of another or is actually bitten by the infected animal, your pet can pick up the virus. But he will be immune if he has been vaccinated. The first shot should be given at six months of age. Boosters should follow if the disease is present in wild or domestic animals in your area.

What are the symptoms of rabies?

Form I, the "furious" form, makes the dog behave hostilely. He may run helter-skelter without reason, grabbing or biting anything or anyone who crosses his path. He may eat flowers, stones, or other inedible items. Form II, the "paralytic" form, makes the animal appear stupid. He foams at the mouth and is unable to swallow anything. He becomes very shy and might hide in a corner.

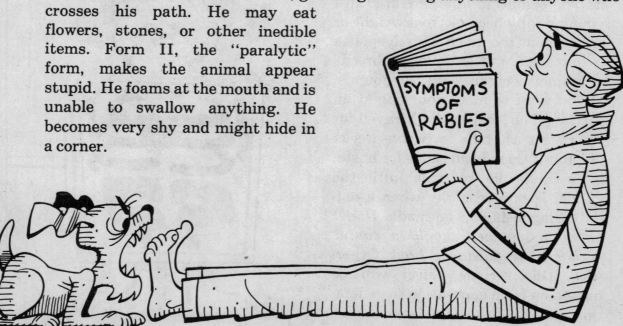

How do you know if your dog has distemper?

Distemper is a virus that can be prevented only through proper vaccinations, followed by annual boosters. Signs of the disease are high fever, loss of appetite, heavy discharge of the nose and eyes, a hacking cough, severe diarrhea, vomiting, and convulsions. In addition, the dog may become blind, partially paralyzed, and lose complete control of his bowels.

If your pet contracts distemper, devoted nursing care is essential. Try to keep your pet in good spirits and make sure he is comfortable, warm, and well groomed. Serve him nourishing food, such as scrambled eggs, chopped beef, and boiled fish, fed a spoonful at a time, and encourage him to drink plenty of water. To prevent his nose from getting too dry, apply mineral oil, and wipe away any discharge from the eyes and nose with warm water. Clean his hindquarters after bowel movements, massage his limbs, and keep the room immaculate. (Even after your pet recovers from distemper—about 30% of the dogs who contract the disease die—his nervous system may be permanently damaged.)

This dreadful disease is not transferable to man. A dog who has survived distemper will have developed antibodies and will be immune to another attack.

179

What do you do if your dog catches hepatitis?

Canine infectious hepatitis is the full name of this disease, and it is not the same type that affects humans, so you cannot catch it. Your dog contracts the disease from the urine or feces of an infected animal, and this is one reason why you should not allow your pet to sniff his way along the road, especially if he has not been vaccinated. Hepatitis usually affects dogs while they are still immature, and it damages both the intestines and liver. Although the onset is rather like distemper, the signs that follow differ. The dog pushes his stomach against the floor and keeps humping his back, trying to relieve the pains. Your pet must be brought to a veterinarian for treatment, although it may not be successful. Again, this horrible, usually fatal, disease rarely occurs if your pet is properly vaccinated at the correct times.

How can you tell if your dog has leptospirosis?

This disease has many of the same symptoms as distemper, but it has its own distinctive signs as well. The dog's urine usually smells pungent and it is orange in color. His temperature will rise and drop rapidly. The dog rarely lies down or stands up; he simply sits. You can catch leptospirosis from your dog, and it can be transferred from dog to dog and especially from rat to dog. Rush your pet to the veterinarian for speedy treatment. If the virus spreads to your pet's liver and kidneys, he may die. This is another disease that can be prevented if your dog is vaccinated at the proper intervals throughout his life.

What is a DHL immunization?

This is a triple vaccine which provides immunity against distemper, hepatitis, and leptospirosis all in one shot. The puppy has immunization from drinking his mother's milk (provided she has been vaccinated). But he should receive his own temporary shots when he is weaned, permanent shots at about three months of age, and an annual booster thereafter.

A dog who has hard paw pads is suffering from a disease almost as serious as distemper. True or False?

This is a form of distemper that may accompany all the other usual symptoms, or may exist on its own. The dog makes a clicking sound as he walks across a floor, and this sound is *not made by his claws* but by the paw pads. Examine them and you will find that they are very hard indeed. The dog may sway, stumble, and fall as if he is drunk. This is because his brain has been affected along with his entire nervous system and, if he does not die, there is little alternative but to have him put to sleep to prevent further suffering.

Your dog lost a leg in an accident. He is in the hospital and the bills are mounting up. Will he recover, or should you terminate his life now?

Dogs run around quite well on three legs, just as if nothing was wrong, and once your dog recovers, he will be unaware of his handicap.

What causes a dog to become paralyzed without any warning?

Sometimes certain ticks carry a paralyzing germ, or the dog may have suffered a fall of which you were unaware. Otherwise, especially if the dog is a Dachshund, Beagle, or any breed with a rather long body, paralysis is caused by the efforts of breeders to make the dog's body excessively long. A structural change in the spinal cord occurs and the discs become overloaded with calcium, causing them to slip out of place and press on the spinal nerves. The result is great pain for the dog and usually paralysis of his hind legs.

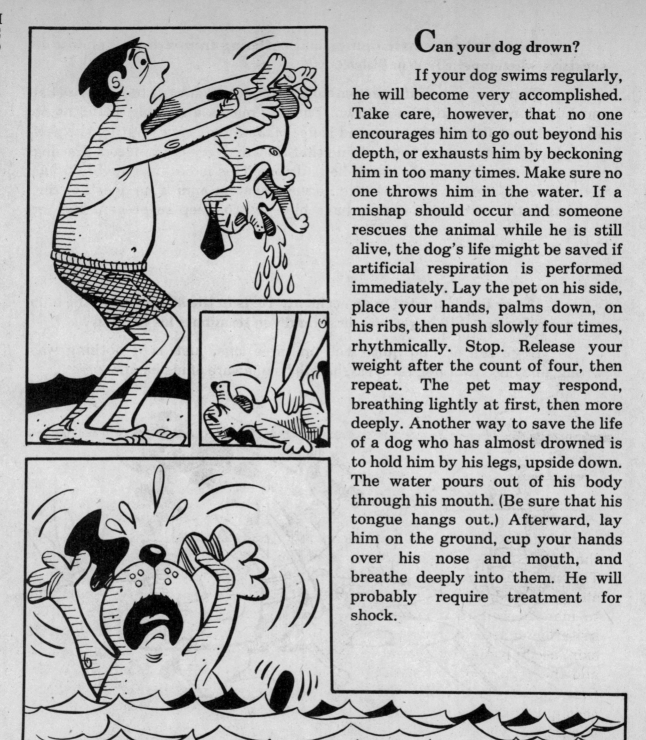

Can your dog drown?

If your dog swims regularly, he will become very accomplished. Take care, however, that no one encourages him to go out beyond his depth, or exhausts him by beckoning him in too many times. Make sure no one throws him in the water. If a mishap should occur and someone rescues the animal while he is still alive, the dog's life might be saved if artificial respiration is performed immediately. Lay the pet on his side, place your hands, palms down, on his ribs, then push slowly four times, rhythmically. Stop. Release your weight after the count of four, then repeat. The pet may respond, breathing lightly at first, then more deeply. Another way to save the life of a dog who has almost drowned is to hold him by his legs, upside down. The water pours out of his body through his mouth. (Be sure that his tongue hangs out.) Afterward, lay him on the ground, cup your hands over his nose and mouth, and breathe deeply into them. He will probably require treatment for shock.

Is tartar accumulation hazardous to the dog's teeth?

Yes. The tartar will push the teeth away from the gums, and the teeth may fall out. Tartar build-up will also give your dog foul breath. If the damage is too extensive to be cured by gnawing bones or rawhide toys, ask the vet to thoroughly clean your pet's teeth. The dog will need anesthesia for this.

The dog has swollen gums and a big bump under his eye that is sensitive when touched. What is wrong?

He probably has an absessed tooth, and it will have to be extracted. It must be done by a vet who has the proper equipment to pull teeth and to administer anesthesia.

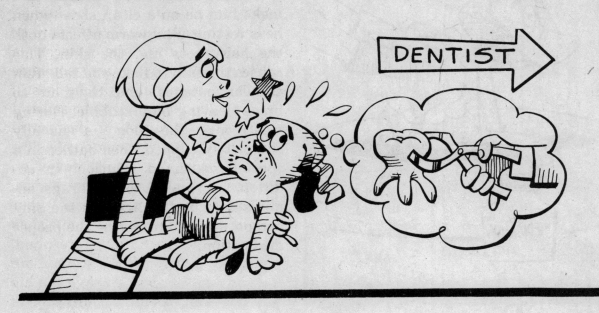

What is mange and how can you tell if your dog has it?

Mange is caused by mites. There are two types, and they are commonly called "red mange" and "scabies." Red mange becomes evident when the dog displays hairless spots on his front legs, neck, muzzle, and eye area. The skin on these bare patches is inflamed and pimply. If the disease is allowed to progress, his entire coat will succumb. Scabies is highly contagious to man as well as to other dogs. The dog scratches furiously due to the irritation caused by red spots, scabs, and a thickening and wrinkling of the skin, accompanied by a great loss of fur. The ears are usually badly infected, and the dog's constant scratching may cause a secondary infection. Scabies first appears around the dog's shoulders, neck, ears, and the top of the head, then quickly spreads all over the body. Both types of mange are very difficult to cure, so a veterinarian must take charge of the case.

What causes eczema?

Eczema, another skin disorder, can be caused by overheating, parasites, allergy to a rug or new food, or dampness. In any case, the dog will scratch the red patches (whether they are moist or dry), making the condition worse if his claws are dirty. And he may lose his fur. Apply some calamine lotion to soothe the areas, then take your pet to the vet for further treatment.

What is ringworm and is it contagious?

Ringworm, a skin disease, is extremely contagious. Wear gloves when handling your animal and make him lie on a clean sheet when he is resting. Ringworm affects both the hair roots and the skin. This causes the skin to flake and fall off in circular patches, and the hair to break, leaving only stubble. During treatment, the dog is usually completely clipped, then bathed in a special medicated solution. In addition, he receives other drugs administered orally. A vet is the only person who can prescribe the proper medication.

Does a dull coat signify a sick dog?

A lusterless coat is one of the signs that your dog is not in top-notch condition. However, if you have been neglecting his grooming, give him extra brushings and combings, and add the yoke of a cooked egg to his food every day. (Do not use the white of the egg; this might make matters worse.) But if you *have* been taking care of his fur, take your pet to the vet for a check-up.

The veterinarian said that your sick dog must not sleep in your room because the dog's illness was "zoonotic." What does this mean?

Zoonotic, pronounced zoh-on-ot-tic, means that your dog is suffering from a disease that is communicable to humans. Actually, there are far more diseases that man can transmit to an animal than the other way around, so sleeping separately is a good idea when either you or your dog is sick.

Can dogs fake illness?

Yes. They sometimes pretend they are sick to gain attention, especially if they have had an injury in the past and received a great deal of pampering. Even though the dog is healthy, give in to his bids for a little extra attention.

Your dog has developed a large lump in his abdomen. Could it be cancerous?

Take your dog to the vet. He will perform a biopsy—the removal of a small piece of tissue to be examined for cancerous cells. If the dog is young and has a cancerous tumor that is removed in time, he may live out his life without further trouble. If the tumor is not malignant, the dog may live with the tumor, provided it does not interfere with the functioning of his other internal organs. If the dog is very old, many owners feel it is best not to subject the dog to an operation and the period of recovery that follows. These owners leave the animal untouched until he experiences pain or great discomfort, and then they have him put to sleep. Medical research for the treatment of tumors with injections is being conducted, and perhaps sometime in the near future, surgery will be unnecessary.

Your Dog's Legal Rights

NO DOGS ALLOWED!

Is there a legal length for a dog leash?

Indeed there is a prescribed length for a leash. In most cities and states, it must not be longer than 6 feet, preventing the dog from becoming entangled in it and seriously injured. If the dog is tied to something, the 6-foot leash also hinders high jumps. A leash that is too short is just as dangerous; it can result in the animal choking himself, or actually cutting his own throat if a chain leash is worn.

Must you keep your animal on a leash?

Most areas have laws clearly stating that you are required to control your dog in this manner. It is sensible to keep your pet on his leash because he can jump on strangers, frightening or hurting them, run out into traffic, defecate in unsuitable places, breed haphazardly, or be "dognapped."

Some owners have fought and won the right to keep their dogs in apartments even though their leases specifically forbid it. True or False?

An organization in New York City has successfully fought many such cases on the grounds that the tenants needed the dogs for security, and the wording in the lease referring to dog ownership represented a minimal part of the agreement and was insufficient cause for eviction. As a result of this, landlords are now revising their leases and are unquestionably forbidding tenants to own animals.

If your landlord *does* forbid animals in your building, it is not advisable to try to own one secretly, because if the truth is revealed, the landlord can take legal action against you, and force you to move or find a new home for your dog, which will be difficult to do if he is over three years of age—not as readily adoptable as a puppy.

The landlord permits you to have a dog in your apartment. If he changes his mind or sells the house to a new owner, is there anything you can do to protect your right to keep the dog?

Insist that your lease include a clause clearly stating your rights to keep a dog in your apartment under any circumstances. In my own apartment house, a new landlord bought the building and all tenants were required to give up their pets with the exception of those who had such a clause included in their leases. In many states, later leases *must* conform to the terms of the original lease.

The neighbors complain because your dog barks all day. Can they take any legal steps against you?

Yes. They can have your dog declared a nuisance. You would then have to move or find a new home for him.

Can a beggar obtain a Seeing Eye Dog?

Seeing Eye Dog is the registered trademark of the institution of that name. They scientifically breed the dogs and train them and their prospective owners properly. One of the regulations that is strictly enforced is that no person who receives a Seeing Eye Dog may beg or use the dog for the purpose of obtaining money. So, any dog seen with a beggar cannot have been supplied by the Seeing Eye Dog institution and should be referred to as a guide dog.

You sold some dog beds and now the buyer wants his money back. He says it is illegal to resell these items. Is this true?

It is against the law to sell used bedding. But if you remove the cushions and throw them away and wash the metal or straw part before resale, you would not be doing anything out of order, according to the law in most areas.

Is it illegal to photograph a dog that does not belong to you and enter the photo in a photography contest?

If you wish to photograph a dog, with or without his owner, you should first ask permission. Usually the person approached is proud and delighted to have his dog's picture taken, but if he isn't, you should not take the picture. If it is a practice of yours to take dog pictures, prepare a release for the owner to sign, in which he agrees that he does not object to you taking or using his dog's picture. As a courtesy, you might want to send a copy of the picture to the dog owner if you win the contest and the photo is published. These suggestions apply only to amateurs and hobbyists. Never feature the dog's photograph in an advertisement for a commercial product unless the proper legal steps have been taken.

Your dog bit a friend and she went to the doctor for a tetanus shot. The doctor reported this case to the health department. Was this necessary?

The doctor is legally obligated to report a dog bite to your city's health department. Sometimes this brings the local dog warden or policeman to your door, and you might be ordered to place your dog under the supervision of a veterinarian for ten days.

The dog has bitten two people. If he bites another person, he must be put to death. True or False?

In many large cities, the dog must be put to death after his third biting offense, whether he is to blame or not.

The dog was outside alone for his usual morning walk and was rounded up by the men of the local animal shelter, and they charged a fee for his release. Is this customary?

If your dog is picked up because he is outside without a leash, it is in accordance with general practice to charge a fee for his release.

How much authority does the pound keeper have?

He is an appointed public officer and required to carry out his duties in accordance with the laws governing the area under his jurisdiction. He is concerned with the well being and protection of your dog, and his position should be respected. If you wrongfully interfere with his responsibilities, he has the legal right to bring charges against you for "obstructing him in the course of his duties."

Is there insurance to protect you from being sued if your dog bites someone?

There is no specific policy available right now, but a regular comprehensive personal liability policy or homeowners policy often supplies this protection for injuries to anyone other than members of your immediate family. Ask your insurance agent if clauses can be written into your policy to assure you of appropriate coverage.

Are there any statistics on dog bite wounds?

Yes, although of course they vary from year to year. At last reporting, the ASPCA stated that approximately 600,000 people in the United States—35,728 people in New York City alone—suffered bite wounds in the past year. However, it is believed that about twice as many cases occur that are never reported.

The dog warden came for your dog after he bit someone, but you couldn't find your pet at the time. What should you do now?

Continue your search for the dog and report to the dog warden immediately upon finding him. Otherwise, patrol cars will be on the lookout for your dog as a rabies suspect and the injured person will have to undergo painful rabies shots. If the authorities find your dog first, they may mistakenly believe he has rabies and destroy him.

How can you defend your dog against a bite accusation?

Try to provide reasons why the dog may have bitten the person. Perhaps the victim teased your pet, stepped on his paw, or thrusted his hand in your dog's face, and find a witness who can attest to the act. Also supply sufficient evidence—perhaps with character witnesses—that the dog has always been tame in the past.

If you lose your dog, what authorities should you contact?

Get in touch with all humane societies and animal shelters first: then inform the state and local police; the town or city clerk; town, city, or county dog warden; and any voluntary agencies that find lost dogs. In addition, make photo copies of your dog's picture, identifying his name and your name and address, and stating a sum as a reward. Give this information to all agencies you contact and post it on your gate or in your apartment house elevator and laundry room, in supermarkets, on community bulletin boards, and so on.

Your neighbor claims that your dog broke his window and is suing you for damages. Does he have the right to do this?

If he can prove that your dog is responsible for this act and it has caused him any loss, you may have to pay the amount he requests or the amount decreed by the court.

Friendly Fred, your Miniature Poodle, bit someone who stepped on his paw. Since you had a "BEWARE OF THE DOG" sign showing a vicious looking monster with a spiked collar and snarling teeth in your window, the man is claiming damages because he said you knew your dog was vicious. Is he right?

The "BEWARE OF THE DOG" sign will probably do you in. Under the law, you are responsible for the actions of your dog if you are aware of his behavioral tendencies. If the case goes to court, tell your story to the judge; perhaps he will see your point of view.

Is it true that a police or health officer can order a dog to be put to sleep without the consent of his owner?

In special circumstances, yes. In the United States, the public's rights to be protected comes before the rights of an individual person. Therefore, if it is believed that your dog has a disease that endangers the health of other people or animals, or he is a known biter, the police can take corrective action.

Your St. Bernard had a litter of seven pups and you kept them all. The neighbors are objecting, and are threatening to take legal action if you fail to get rid of your dogs. Can they do this?

Yes. Most residential areas have zoning laws limiting the pets in a household to a specified number. Zoning laws have been enacted to restrict the establishment of kennels in neighborhoods whose property value could be lowered and the peace and quiet of residents disturbed. So check your local laws to find out the maximum number of animals you are permitted to have.

There is a bark collar that gives the dog an electric shock when he makes a noise. Is this legal?

It is legal, and some owners feel it is wiser to train a dog for a short time with one of these than face the possibility of being evicted from their building. However, some people believe this kind of training is cruel. If you buy a bark collar, place it against your own neck and try to estimate if the shock strength is too severe for the size of your dog, and examine your dog's neck every day to make sure the collar hasn't damaged his skin.

Your neighbors had two husky pups but couldn't maintain them because they grew too large. So these people took the dogs out, tied them to a fence in a local park, hoping that someone would take them home. Is this illegal?

In many states, a person who is aware of "an act of abandonment" can sign a complaint against the guilty party, who then may be ordered to pay a fine and even sent to jail. (In New Jersey, for example, the fine is $250, the prison sentence, six months.)

194

You are getting divorced and your wife is taking the dog. Is it possible for you to obtain some visitation rights?

Your lawyer can prepare a separate document stating your wishes, or you can add a few paragraphs relating to this subject in any agreement you make with regard to division of property. Or you can write something yourself and it will be legally binding, provided you and your wife and two witnesses who are not related to you sign it. The document should include the following:

- Your name, your wife's name, and the name of the dog (or dogs).

- A brief description of the dog, breed, age, and so on.

- A provision that the dog is to be kept by your wife, but if she should die, remarry, move away, or whatever terms you'd like to set, the dog must go to you. Also a statement that she must not sell, give away, or have the dog put to sleep without your permission.

- An explanation of the visitation terms. For instance, you may have the dog every weekend; she is to return the dog to you when she goes on vacation; she must never take the dog out of the state, etc.

- A statement that should your wife be unable to care for the dog, for whatever reason, she must offer the dog to you.

- A declaration of financial responsibility for the dog's food, maintenance, medicine, boarding, and burial expenses.

- A stipulation of how the fees shall be split if the dog is used as a stud or bears pups.

Are dogs banned anywhere?

Indeed they are! Reykjavik (Iceland), Singapore (Malaysia), parts of London, and many oriental countries, to name but a few places, have banned dogs. Roosevelt Island (New York City), described as "a model for future American cities," has a similar ban. The only way to prevent such a law from being passed where you live is to make a giant effort to keep your dog under your control at all times. Otherwise, the day may come when the only place you will be able to see a West Highland Terrier, French Poodle, or Cocker Spaniel is in the zoo.

Show Time

- **American Kennel Club Competitions**
- **Obedience Trials**
- **Mongrels in Competition**
- **Field Trials**
- **Benched and Unbenched Shows**
- **Winning Titles**
- **Prize Ribbons**

Can a dog be entered in a contest if his coat has been dyed?

If you are entering a dog in an AKC affiliated contest, you must follow their strict rules and regulations concerning your particular breed. Generally, alteration in a dog's coloring will eliminate him from competition. In an unofficial, local show run by a charitable organization, entrants are not scrutinized as closely, especially if the judge is a celebrity who has primarily been hired to draw crowds.

Can a mongrel be entered in competition?

There are dog shows run by county fairs, animal shelters, and charitable organizations that allow mongrels to be entered in competition for "The Cutest Dog," "The Cleverest Dog," "The Most Intelligent Dog," "The Most Beautiful Dog," among other categories. Ask your local animal organization and look for announcements on the pet pages of your local newspaper for information about these competitions.

Who runs obedience trials?

Some obedience trials are AKC affiliated competitions, while others are sponsored by dog training schools or charitable organizations. If the AKC does not sanction the show, your dog will not earn any official credits, but he might win a ribbon or certificate for a fine performance. If you enjoy these events and are not interested in serious competition, they provide you with a goal when training your pet. Should you later wish to enter into fierce competition on a higher level, both you and your dog will have gained valuable experience in the show arena.

How can you find the dates of upcoming obedience shows?

Dog World magazine publishes regular listings of all upcoming events, and you can ask the AKC to place your name on mailing lists for material on local and national competitions. Your local newspaper will also advertise important AKC events as well as fun shows, so keep an eye on the pet pages.

What is a field trial and what is expected of a dog when he competes in one?

Field trials are competitions held to encourage breeding of hounds, sporting dogs, gun dogs, bird dogs, and retrievers, and they strive to upgrade performance in the field. Spaniels can also enter these contests. Instead of judging animals on their physical attributes, the field trial judge judges them on performance. Exercises vary according to the breed of dog involved. For instance, hounds which follow furred game must use their noses in order to detect the scent of the game, then give tongue (bay) when trailing. Bird dogs must find birds, hold a steady point (points to the source of the scent with his head and tail held high, and then freezes in position), provide a reliable backup for their running mates, and remain stationary when a bird takes flight and the shot is fired. Retrievers are expected to plunge into ice-cold rivers or rush into thick underbrush in order to fetch a bird or animal. Spaniels must find birds, flush them into the open where they can be seen, then retrieve the bodies after they have been shot.

How do you know where and when field trials will be held?

This information can be found in sporting and hunting magazines. Write to the clubs that usually sponsor these events and ask to be placed on their mailing lists. You will probably find that in a short time, you will be receiving information about field trials as well as many other allied activities.

Would you enjoy watching a field trial?

FIELD TRIAL HANDBOOK

HORSES FOR RENT

You may find it a thrilling and rewarding experience, but wear a pair of sturdy shoes and take binoculars. Usually, there is no admission charge and horses are available for rent. So if you can ride, you will be able to keep up with the action. It is an exciting time to watch the marvelous dogs running swiftly (alone or in unison with others), pointing, retrieving, and displaying their fine skill and intelligence. Many animal lovers frown upon these activities because there is killing involved, but the events continue to be popular among hunters and sportsmen.

What is the difference between a benched show and an unbenched show?

At a benched show, entrants spend most of their time in numbered stalls, with their owners and handlers usually sitting nearby. An unbenched show often takes place outdoors, sometimes under a big tent. There are no stalls and the dogs often remain in crates or in the backs of cars awaiting their turn in the show ring. If it is a damp day, the grounds often become very muddy, so if you attend an unbenched show, wear sturdy, watertight shoes.

What's so special about Crufts and the Westminster Kennel Club Show?

They are the most famous dog shows in the world. Crufts takes place in England, the Westminster Kennel Club Annual Dog Show, in New York City. The latter, usually held the second week in February, has about 3,000 canines entered in its competitions. If you attend this event, buy a guidebook, visit the dogs in their stalls, watch them being beautified in the grooming area, and follow their progress in the show ring. You will enjoy it thoroughly and learn a great deal. But unless you want to buy a particular dam's pups (which are often on display) or are seriously interested in some other business transaction with the owner or handlers, do not bother them with trivial questions because they are under considerable tension, competing against the finest dogs in the country.

What do the different colored ribbons indicate in an AKC sponsored competition?

Ribbon	Title
• Purple and gold	Best of Breed or Best of Variety of Breed
• Red and white	Best of Opposite Sex
• Blue and white	Best of Litters
• Purple and white	Best of Reserve Litters
• Solid blue	First prize for Obedience
• Solid red	Second prize for Obedience
• Solid yellow	Third prize for Obedience
• Solid white	Fourth prize for Obedience
• Dark green	Special prize (Best Stud, Best Bitch, etc.)
• Any elaborate combination of colors that do not duplicate any of the above	Best in Show

Each of the rosettes with ribbons attached must be 2 inches wide and 8 inches in length. Also, each must bear the imprint of the kennel club, the name of the prize, the name of the club running the event, the date of the contest, and the city and town where the event took place.

What are the rules for entering AKC contests?

The regulations are long and exceedingly detailed but vitally important to those who are entering dogs in competitions. Obtain a copy from the AKC and don't skip a word if you are interested in serious competition.

Some dogs have letters that appear before or after their names. What do they mean?

• *C.D. = Companion Dog:* He has earned at least 170 points out of a possible 200 in three separate obedience trials in the novice category. Usually, three different judges have awarded him these points while he performed on-leash most of the time.

• *C.D.X. = Companion Dog Excellent:* This animal has won 170 points or more out of a maximum of 200 in three obedience trials held on three different occasions, usually in front of three different judges. In every case, his performance was off-leash.

• *U.D. = Utility Dog:* This dog already had a C.D. or C.D.X. and then competed in the utility class where he won at least 170 points out of a maximum 200 in three different obedience trials where he probably performed in front of three different judges.

• *U.D.T. = Utility Dog Tracker:* After being awarded a C.D.X. and U.D., two AKC approved judges permitted the dog to compete against at least three other dogs in this quarter-mile outdoor contest. This is the most prestigious obedience title a dog can be awarded.

• *Ch. = Champion:* This dog has won a maximum of five points awarded by three different judges at three different bench shows. Thus, he has won the necessary fifteen points to become a champion.

• *Dual Ch. = Dual Champion:* This dog has become a champion in bench shows and has competed and won a field trial championship.

In all cases, the AKC sets the point schedule. It may vary from time to time for dogs and bitches of the same breed, and it may be altered to suit the conditions of different parts of the country.

What exercises must a dog perform when competing in obedience trials?

- **To earn his C.D. (mostly on-leash):** Points
  1. Heel on-leash — 35
  2. Stand for examination by judge — 30
  3. Heel off-leash — 45
  4. Recall — 30
  5. Long sit (1 minute) — 30
  6. Long down (1 minute) — 30

  Maximum total score — 200 points

- **To earn his C.D.X. (off-leash):** Points
  1. Heel off-leash — 40
  2. Drop on recall — 30
  3. Retrieve on flat ground — 25
  4. Retrieve after high jump — 35
  5. Broad jump — 20
  6. Long sit (3 minutes) — 25
  7. Long down (3 minutes) — 25

  Maximum total score — 200 points

- **To earn his U.D.:**   **Points**

		Points
1.	Scent discrimination Article #1	30
2.	Scent discrimination Article #2	30
3.	Directed retrieve	30
4.	Signal exercise	35
5.	Directed jumping	40
6.	Group examination	35

          Maximum total score — 200 points

- **To earn his U.D.T.:**

Follow a human's trail for at least a quarter of a mile across country.

If the dog fails to respond the first time a command is given, he loses all his points for that particular exercise.

The Older Dog and When the End Comes

- **Common Ailments of the Older Dog**
- **The Older Dog's Coat**
- **Intestinal Disorders**
- **Exercise**
- **Eyesight and Hearing**
- **Preparing for Your Dog's Death**
- **Putting Your Dog to Sleep**
- **Burials and Cremation**

What are the most common ailments of elderly dogs?

- *Kidney disease:* Most old dogs suffer from kidney disease. Symptoms are bad breath, little or no appetite, scraggy hair, vomiting, diarrhea, frequent urination, and great thirst.

- *Heart disease:* If your dog tires easily, or pants excessively after exercise, he may have a heart disorder. Other symptoms are coughing and fainting spells. Do not let him become overweight—excess weight will increase the burden on an ailing heart.

- *Arthritis:* This is characterized by stiffness in the elbows, knees, spine, and hip joint.

- *Enlargement of the prostate gland:* Enlargement of the prostate gland is common in older dogs of the male sex. There may be blood in the stool, difficulty in passing stool, frequent urinating, or difficulty in urinating.

- *Inflamed uterus:* Unspayed, unbred females are usually afflicted. Indications of its presence are vaginal discharge, swollen abdomen, excessive thirst, and little or no appetite.

- *Overweight:* This is something you must control. As your pet grows older, the size of his meals should be cut down. Continue to exercise him every day, even though he may not romp as much as in his earlier years.

Now that your dog is older, his coat doesn't shine. Is there something you can do to make him look better?

The older dog's skin glands become less active, resulting in less sheen to his coat. Groom him daily, but don't expect the results to be as satisfying as when he was young.

Will your dog turn grey as he ages?

He will not turn grey, but white hairs will appear, usually on the top of his head and around his muzzle. Single white hairs often crop up throughout the entire coat.

Your dog has trouble emptying his bowels. Can he be helped?

This condition of old age can be eased by giving your dog sufficient exercise and some milk of magnesia every three days (1/2 teaspoon for every 5 pounds of his weight). If this doesn't help, take your pet to a veterinarian.

Your pet is very old and suffers from diarrhea. Is this normal?

This is not really normal, but various changes do occur in the bowels during a pet's later years. Give him Kaopectate every three days (1/2 teaspoon for every 5 pounds of his weight). Increase the dose if it appears to be helping but not quite enough. If the condition persists, however, take him to the vet. Your pet may be suffering from kidney disease or a tumor in the intestines.

What can you do for the aging pet with a weak bladder?

Your pet can't retain his urine because his sphincter muscle has weakened due to old age. Take him out regularly and often. Put a plastic sheet covered with soft blankets over his bedding. He can't control himself, and, unfortunately, there is nothing more you can do.

The dog has developed painful, hard patches on his elbows. What can you do to ease his discomfort?

Massage the dog's elbows with mineral oil, then gently comb out the flattened hair. He will find this very soothing. In addition, if he is accustomed to lying on something hard, encourage him to rest on a blanket or rug.

Your hound is old and his legs are swollen. What is wrong?

Press the swelling with your fingers. If you indent the flesh and it remains that way for thirty seconds or more, he probably has an edema (abnormal excess accumulation of fluid in the tissues). Take him to the vet immediately.

Should an older dog be exercised?

An older dog should not be encouraged to take part in vigorous exercises he has never enjoyed during his younger years. Anything he has done before is fine, although he may do it more slowly.

Your family pet is ten years old and in great shape. What can you do to keep him fit?

Feed him specially prepared food for older dogs, and bring him to the vet for a check-up every year. Be understanding if he starts to slow down, but don't let him become lazy and fat. Encourage him to exercise, but don't urge furious activity.

What can you do for the dog who has become blind?

Pedestrians will not know your pet is blind, so they may be offended if he walks into them, or they may step on his toes if he doesn't get out of their way. Try to walk your pet when there are few people around and talk to him so he doesn't feel insecure. He should always be on a leash when outdoors. In the home, don't rearrange the furniture, or leave anything around that your pet could accidently bump into.

Should you allow your old dog to cross the street by himself?

An animal's eyes change with age, limiting his vision. He may also become slightly deaf and his reflexes may not react as quickly as they once did. Your pet should not be unaccompanied outside at any age, especially if he is an older dog.

Your dog has glaucoma. Is glaucoma hereditary?

Yes. And it rarely skips a generation. This is why it is unkind to breed an animal when it is known that he has a hereditary defect. However, since glaucoma does not usually become apparent until the dog's later years, the breeder may not have been aware of the condition.

What can you do to ensure the safety of a deaf dog?

When outdoors, always keep your deaf dog on a leash, protecting him from bicycles and cars that he cannot hear approaching. Indoors, have patience if he doesn't come when you call. Usually, when one sense is lost, the others become more keen, and to a certain extent, compensate for the defect. For instance, if you open the door before walking your pet, he might feel the draft and understand that it is time to go out. Or he might smell your dinner cooking and realize that it is time for him to eat too. Your dog will adjust to his loss of hearing and function reasonably well.

Your pet walks very, very stiffly and often whimpers in pain when he lies down. What is wrong?

Your dog probably has arthritis. Give him 1/8 of an aspirin for every 5 pounds of his weight (but no more than two aspirins) every five hours. If possible, let him lie on an electric blanket set on a low temperature. This should ease his discomfort.

When your dog died, his tongue was hanging out and it was pitch black. Did he die of a terrible disease?

No. When a dog's diet has been deficient in niacin during his lifetime, his tongue will turn black after death. But don't feel guilty; the dog did not die because he did not have enough niacin.

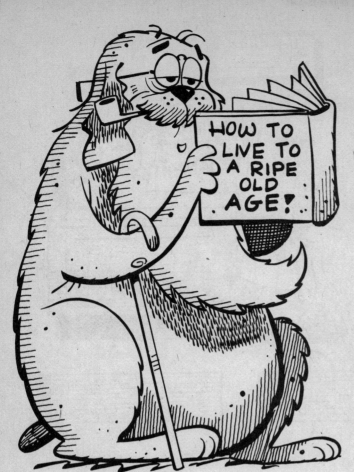

What is the average lifespan of a dog?

The average lifespan is about fourteen years, although it is not uncommon for a dog to die from old age a year or two earlier, and, in rare cases, a year or two later. Some breeds tend to live longer than others. Generally, larger breeds have shorter lives, smaller breeds, longer ones.

Should you allow an autopsy to be performed on your dog?

If your dog dies of an undiagnosed ailment which puzzles the veterinarians, it would be beneficial to allow an autopsy. The information gained may save other dogs from the same lethal disease.

Should you make preparations for your dog's death?

It is very sensible to prepare for your dog's death in advance. Plan the arrangements for his burial, write them down, and give them to a friend or relative. This way, someone will have instructions in case you are not home when the dog dies.

If you die before your pet does, how can you make sure he will receive proper care and a suitable burial?

Have your lawyer add a paragraph to your will stating the care and burial you wish your dog to receive, to be paid for with money you have left expressly for this purpose.

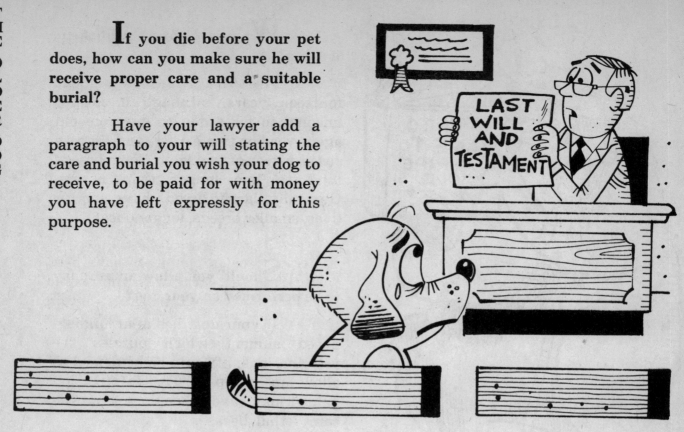

What is the simplest way to dispose of your pet's body after he has passed away?

Call your local sanitation department. They will tell you how and where to leave the body. Wrap the pet in something that isn't transparent, but tell the sanitation department you plan to do this so they know what to look for when they come to collect the pet. Many people fail to cover the dog, and their last vision of their pet lying on the sidewalk next to a garbage can is very disheartening.

When you bring your pet to the veterinarian to have him put to sleep, how can you be sure it is done?

Unless your dog would be an extremely valuable specimen, it is unlikely that the vet would ignore your request. However, if you want to be sure, you can ask the vet to permit you to watch. You will see that your dog dies painlessly within seconds.

What is the best way to put your dog to sleep?

Take your pet to a veterinarian who has a private practice and a crematorium. He will put the dog to sleep with the proper injection and cremate the animal on his own premises under his supervision.

Can a large animal institution put your pet to sleep?

They can, but it is not advisable. Although the actual death process occurs in seconds, animals are frequently huddled together in a decompression chamber that is filled to capacity. They become frantic while waiting for all the animals to enter, and this final terror is heartless. (In some states, decompression chambers have been outlawed, so check with the animal institution in your area to ascertain what method they use.) A smaller institution that has fewer strays to cope with might be able to put each animal to sleep one at a time.

Why do large humane societies destroy so many animals at the same time?

In large cities, there are many, many strays and unwanted animals that must be disposed of every day, and there is no other way to do it, considering the number that must be treated. This is why spaying and neutering are so important, and indiscriminate breeding, cruel.

Will the local animal shelter dispose of your dog properly?

A local animal shelter that regularly destroys animals that have been abandoned will probably allow you to deliver your pet to their premises or, for a fee, pick him up from your home. He will be placed among the day's unwanteds and disposed of in the same fashion as they are. If there are large numbers of animals put to death at this institution, it is likely that the bodies are picked up two or three times a week by industrial companies who process their remains.

Can you cremate your dog and keep the ashes?

Some animal associations will perform this service for a fee. Otherwise, you must find a veterinarian who has the necessary facilities or go to an animal cemetery that has a crematorium.

Is it possible to purchase a cemetery plot for your animal while he is still alive?

Yes. Plots usually measure about 2 feet by 3 feet to 2 feet by 5 feet. Generally, each plot accommodates two burials, but if the dog is very large, you might need two plots.

How can you arrange the best funeral possible for your pet?

The most elaborate animal cemeteries are on the west coast of the United States. However, there are some highly dignified and expensive ones in other parts of the country. Try to visit two or three cemeteries, or at least obtain brochures well in advance of need. Choices vary, but you will usually have to make decisions about the following:

• *Transportation:* Will they pick up the deceased animal? Will you be allowed to accompany the corpse in the same car? If yes, will you be returned to your home again?

• *Plot:* How many bodies can be placed in one plot? Can you choose its location? Is it cemetery policy to mow over the plots and use them again. If so, in how many years?

• *Storage vault:* If the body cannot be buried right away (perhaps because you are on vacation), is there a storage vault on the premises?

• *Ceremony:* Will the cemetery association arrange for a ceremony? Is it permissable to conduct your own last rites if you wish?

• *Casket:* Can you bury the dog without a casket? If a casket is necessary (it most likely will be), what types are available? (Choices may vary from an inexpensive casket, which is made of plywood and lined with thin cloth, to a lined pine casket, which is a bit more expensive, to a deluxe casket, which is usually redwood and upholstered with foam rubber covered with colored satin.)

• *Marker:* How will the grave be identified? Sometimes only a uniform metal marker that bears the number of the plot is allowed. Otherwise, there is a variety of choices. You can select a flat memorial tablet, an upright stone, a large tomb (perhaps to accommodate several dogs), an obelisk, and more, made of fine marble or expensive granite. An inset of your dog's picture or any words you wish to engrave can be placed on your choice.

• *Maintenance:* Is maintenance available? Will flowers be planted at regular intervals? Is there a one-time perpetual care charge or an annual fee?

If cremation is involved, you will have to consider the following: Will they cremate the animal? Can you take the ashes? Is there a mausoleum where your dog's remains can be housed? What type of urns are available? Are there any extras to consider—a bud vase near the remains? Continuous music? Fountains running day and night in a great marble hall?

Can you bury your dog in the garden?

In many states, it is against the law to bury an animal, even on your own property. Check with the Board of Health in your area. If it is permissable, dig a very deep grave (there should be at least 18 inches of dirt covering the corpse). After burying the pet, pile many rocks on top of the site so that wild animals cannot disturb the grave. Mark the burial spot with something strong and durable and point it out to new tenants if you move away. Otherwise, they might unknowingly unearth the body and become very, very frightened.

How can you perpetuate your dog's memory?

Make a contribution to an animal association, "In memory of (Pet's name)." If you donate a large amount of money, request that the association buy a medical instrument or bank of cages and inscribe on the gift, "In memory of (Pet's name)." Or visit an adoption center where hundreds of beautiful, healthy mongrel and pedigreed dogs await, and rescue one in honor of your departed pet.

Glossary

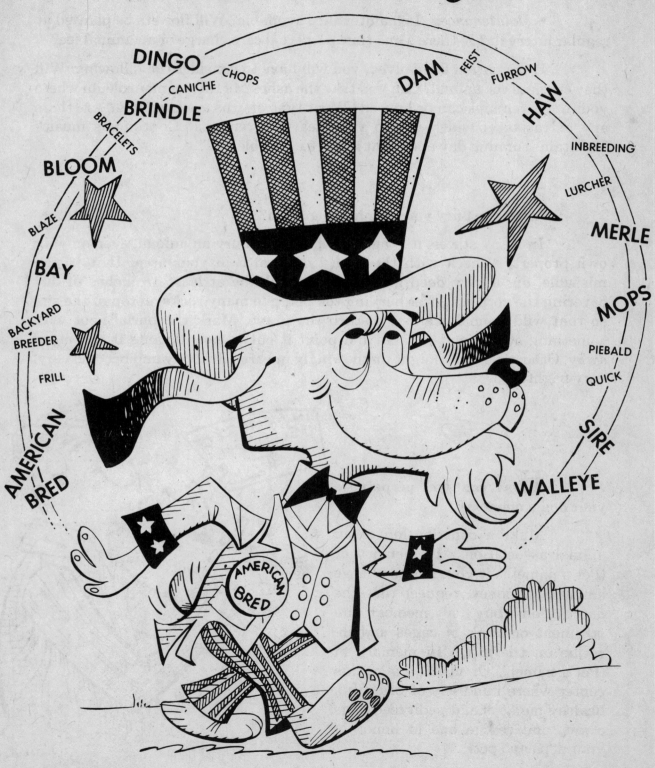

DINGO

CANICHE CHOPS

BRINDLE

BRACELETS

BLOOM

BLAZE

BAY

BACKYARD
BREEDER

FRILL

AMERICAN
BRED

DAM FEIST FURROW

HAW

INBREEDING

LURCHER

MERLE

MOPS

PIEBALD

QUICK

SIRE

WALLEYE

AMERICAN
BRED

Action: The way a dog walks or runs.

Albino: A dog who does not possess normal coloration. Signs are extremely pale blue or grey eyes, flesh-colored nose, and white coat.

Almond Eye: An oval eye set on a slant. Seen in Bull Terriers.

Alsatian: Synonymous with German Shepherd. The term is more commonly used in England.

Alter/Neuter: To remove reproduction organs so that an animal cannot produce offspring.

American-Bred: A dog born in the United States from a mating which also took place in the United States. (Some people jokingly use this term for their mongrels.)

Amniotic Fluid: The fluid in which an unborn puppy floats while he is being carried inside his mother.

Anal Glands: A pair of organs found on either side of the rectum.

Apple-Headed: A dome-shaped or round skull. Favorable in Toy Spaniels and Chihuahuas. Unsatisfactory in most other breeds.

Apron/Frill: A ruff of long hair found on the dog's throat and chest. Seen in Collies.

Ascob: Abbreviation for "any solid color other than black."

Atavism: The performance of an instinctive act typical of dogs' wild, remote ancestors.

Ataxia: A reeling or staggering walk. Often a sign of brain damage or injury to the spine.

A.V.:   Abbreviation for "any variety." Indicates that show entries are acceptable from any breed, including those who have competed in earlier classes.

A.O.V.:   Abbreviation for "any other variety." Indicates that class entries will be accepted from any canine entrant who has not competed in a previous showing.

B. or b.:	Used in pedigrees and show catalogues to indicate "bitch," the female dog.
B.B.:	Abbreviation for "Best of Breed." In a show, applied to the dog who surpasses all other animals of his own breed.
Backyard Breeder:	An owner who raises litters in his home. (An uncomplimentary term.)

Barrelled:	A reference to the rib cage when it is rounded.
Bat Ears:	Big, pricked, batlike ears. Favorable in French Bulldogs. Unsatisfactory in most other breeds.
Bay:	The voice of a Hound when he's on the trail of the fox or game he is hunting.

Beard: Thick bushy whiskers. Seen in Brussels Griffons.

Belton: A coat of colored and white hairs, such as an orange or blue belton. Seen in English Setters.

Bench: A raised platform divided into stalls which dogs occupy while awaiting their turn in the ring at dog shows.

Bench Show: A show where benching is available for the entrants.

Blanket: A large, dark marking, often black, which is seen on the dog's back and extends to the base of his tail.

Blaze/Flare: An attractive white mark running up the face and between the eyes.

Blocky: 1. A head that is square. Seen in Boston Terriers.
2. A square, chunky body. Seen in Bulldogs.

Bloom: The sheen of a coat that indicates the dog is in tip-top condition.

Blue: A blue-grey coat. Seen in Whippets and Bedlington Terriers.

Brace:
1. Two dogs of the same breed exhibited together.
2. Two dogs who run together in a field trial.

Bracelets: The long hair that encircles the lower part of the leg of a Poodle in one of his special clips.

Breeching:
1. Very long, thick hair on the thighs.
2. The markings on the back and inside of the hind legs of a black and tan dog. Seen in Manchester Terriers and Doberman Pinschers.

Breeder/Br.: The owner of the female at the time the female was bred.

Brindle: A coat that is a mixture of dark and light fur. The effect is usually irregular stripes on a grey, black, or brown background.

Brisket: The section of the body in front of the chest and between the front legs.

Broken Color: A coat that is one solid color broken up by hairs, patches, or stripes of a lighter shade.

Broken-Up Face: A foreface that has a receding nose, deep wrinkles, and a projecting lower jaw. Seen in Bulldogs and Pekinese.

Brood Bitch/ Matron: A female dog kept solely for breeding purposes.

Brush: A tail with long bushy hair. Seen in Spitz breeds.

B.S.: Abbreviation for "Best in Show," which applies to a dog who has beaten all other competing dogs in a single show.

Burr: An uneven formation inside the ear.

Butterfly Nose: A two-colored nose. Often black or brown mottled with a flesh color.

Button Ears: Ears which fold over in front so that the inner cavity is covered. Seen in Fox Terriers.

Camel Back/ Carp Back: A dog that appears crippled because his back has too much of a hump.

Caniche/ Moyen: This is the French word for Poodle and in the United States refers to a Poodle whose size is halfway between Miniature and Standard Poodles.

Canine Teeth/ Eye Teeth: Long, pointed, fanglike teeth directly behind the incisors.

Catalogue: Handbook issued by a club that holds a show. It lists the dog's name, owner, breeder, birthdate, parentage, and registration number. It also supplies the names of the judges, times of judging, prizes, and any other pertinent information.

Cat Foot: A compact, short, round foot. The knuckles are high and arched like those of a cat. Seen in English Foxhounds.

Ch.: Abbreviation for "Champion." Used in pedigrees and show catalogues.

Chamois Ear: A thin, very soft ear.

Cheeky/ Filled Up: Cheek muscles that are well developed. Seen in Bulldogs.

China Eyes: Clear, light blue eyes. Seen in some Corgis.

Chops/Flews: Thick, hanging upper lips. Seen in Bulldogs and Bloodhounds.

Claws: Toenails.

Clip:
1. A dog's coat that has been cut in a particular style to conform to his breed standard.
2. To trim or scissor a dog's coat.

Cloddy: A low, thick-set build.

Close-Coupled: Short-bodied or short-backed.

Coat: The fur covering the dog's body.

Colostrum: The first milk produced by the mother after she has given birth.

Cow Hocks: Joints of hind legs that point inward, toward one another. A fault.

Crank Tail: A tail carried down and resembling a crank in shape.

Cropped: Ears that are cut to make them erect, conforming to specific show standards. Seen in Boxers and Great Danes.

Crossbreed: The offspring of parents of two different breeds.

Croup: The area immediately before the root of the tail.

Cryptorchid: An adult male dog whose testicles are retained in the abdominal cavity. A fault.

Cull: To destroy inferior pups shortly after they are born.

Culotte: The feathery hair on the back of a dog's front legs. Seen in Pomeranians, Pekinese, and Schipperkes.

Cushion: A thick, swollen appearance of the upper lip. Seen in Mastiffs and Bulldogs.

D. or d: Abbreviation for the male dog when mentioned in catalogues and pedigrees.

Dam: The female parent of puppies. The term is most applicable when the female is pregnant, giving birth, or nursing her puppies.

Dewclaw: The fifth claw on each foot, which is found on the inside of the leg. Often removed from puppies a few days after birth.

Dewlap: Loose, hanging skin under the chin and throat. Seen in Bloodhounds.

Dimple: A small depression on each side of the chest. Seen in Dachshunds.

Dingo: Wild dog of Australia.

Dishfaced: An indention in the nasal bone, making the nose look as if it is turned up. Seen in Pointers.

228

Docking: Cutting a dog's tail so that is conforms to breed standards. Seen in Cocker Spaniels, Fox Terriers, and other breeds.

Double Coat: Fur that consists of a course outer-coat and a soft, thick under-coat. Seen in Collies and Old English Sheepdogs.

Downfaced: A downward slant of the nose. Seen in Bull Terriers.

Drop Ears: Ears that are soft and hang close to the head.

Dual Ch.: Abbreviation for "Dual Champion" and means the dog is a Champion in both dog show and field trial competitions. Seen in catalogues and pedigrees.

Dudley Nose: A flesh-colored nose.

Ear Fringes: Long, silky hair, that forms a fringe on each ear. Seen in Spaniels and Setters.

Elbows: Joints near the tops of front legs.

Elephant Action: A walk characterized by lumbering and shuffling.

Entropion: A defect in which the eyelids turn inward and the lashes brush against the eyeball, irritating the eyes.

Entry: A dog who is a competitor in an obedience test, dog show, or field trial.

Estrus: See Heat.

Euthanasia: See Put Down.

Expression: A combination of the placement, color, size, and expression of the eyes which indicate a dog's character, emotional makeup, and intelligence. Certain expressions typify particular breeds. For instance, the Fox Terrier's expression is supposed to display fire, life, and intelligence, while the Beagle's expression should be gentle and pleading.

Eye Teeth: See Canine Teeth.

Fall: Long hair hanging over the face. Seen in the Skye Terrier.

Fancier: A person who is interested in breeding and showing dogs, usually of a specific breed.

Fawn: A light golden-tan coat.

Fear Biter: A dog who bites because he is emotionally unstable.

Feathers: Long, silky fringes of hair on the back legs and under the tail. Seen in Irish Setters, Spaniels, and some Sheepdogs.

Feist: A small mongrel of mixed Terrier ancestry.

Felted/Matted Coat: A coat that has been neglected, becoming matted and wadded. Seen in Cocker Spaniels.

Fiddle Front: Crooked or bandy front legs. The elbows turn out, the pasterns turn in, and the feet turn out. A fault.

Fiddle Head: A long head similar in appearance to a wolf's head.

Filled Up: See Cheeky.

Firehouse Dog: The Dalmatian.

231

Flare: See Blaze.

Flecked: A coat that is spotted with another color.

Flews: See Chops.

Flush: A dog's approach to game birds, causing them to fly high into the sky.

Fly Ears: Ears that point in the wrong directions.

Foreface: The section of the face from the nose tip to the eyes.

Frill: See Apron.

Frog Face: A face with a receding lower jaw and overshot teeth. Seen in Boxers and Boston Terriers.

Front: The view of the front legs and forepart of the body.

Full Eyes: Slightly protruding, round eyes.

Full Mantle Dog: A dog with an area of solid dark fur covering his neck, shoulders, back, and sides. Seen in St. Bernards.

Furrow: A groove in the center of the skull.

Gait: Manner of walking, running, or trotting.

**Gay Tail/
Lofty Tail:**   A tail that is carried straight up.

Gestation: Period of pregnancy (60–65 days).

Giving Tongue: Baying when on the trail of game.

Goose Rump: A rump that slopes from the hip bones to the root of the tail. A fault.

Grizzle: An iron-grey coat color.

Guide Dog: A dog especially trained to guide a blind person.

Gun Dogs: A dog trained to work with its master in finding live game and retrieving game that has been shot (Setters, Retrievers, Pointers, and Spaniels).

Gun Shy: A sporting dog who is afraid of the gun or the sound of a gun being fired.

Handler: The person who takes the dog into the show ring or is in charge of him at an obedience or field trial.

Hard-Mouthed: A gun dog who damages the game he retrieves. A fault.

Harefoot: A long and narrow foot like that of a rabbit.

Harelip: An upper lip with a running slit in the middle to the nose. A fault from which most pups die because they cannot nurse, and a sound basis for putting them to sleep immediately after they are born.

Haunches: Back portion of the thighs on which the dog sits.

Haw: The inner part of the lower eyelid, which is usually red and hangs down. Seen in Bloodhounds and St. Bernards.

Heat/Estrus: The period of ovulation during which a female dog desires mating and the time when conception can occur.

Height: The measurement of the dog from the ground to the top of one shoulder.

Hocks: The joints of the hind legs, similar to the human ankles.

Hucklebones: The top of the hip joints.

Import: A dog born in another country and brought into the United States.

Inbreeding: The mating of closely related animals in order to perpetuate certain desirable traits.

Incisors: Small, even teeth situated in the front of the mouth, used for biting.

Iris: Colored portion of the eye.

Keel: The base of the body. Applied to Dachshunds.

Kink Tail: A sharply bent tail.

Kissing Spots: Different-colored markings on cheeks. Seen in several of the Toy breeds.

Knee: The joint of the front leg.

Lay Back:	A dog's nose that recedes into the face. Seen in Bulldogs.
Leather:	The skin of the soft, hanging ears of some breeds. Seen in Foxhounds, Dachshunds, and Bloodhounds.
Lengthy:	Long in body.

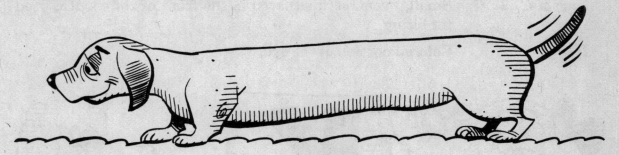

Licensed Show:	Show held under AKC regulations. Points may be collected from such shows and applied toward a championship title.
Line Breeding:	Mating of dogs of similar strain who are not closely related.

Litter:	Family of pups produced by the same mother and born at the same time.
Liver:	A reddish-brown coat color.
Loaded:	A dog that is too heavy in the neck and shoulders.
Lofty Tail:	See Gay Tail.
Loin:	The section of the body between the last rib and the hips.
Low-Set Ears:	Ears that have grown more to the side rather than on top of the head.

Lumber: Excess flesh and weight, which make dogs ungainly in appearance.

Lurcher: A recognized English crossbreed (Greyhound and Sheepdog) now possibly extinct. Lurchers were purposely bred by hunters and gypsies to catch rabbits. Now that the rabbit population has declined, Lurchers are no longer perpetuated.

Maiden: A female dog who has not produced any pups.

Mane: Long hair on the throat and neck.

Mask: A darker coloration of fur on the nose.

Match Show: An informal event where dogs are not awarded any points that can be applied toward AKC championship status.

Matron: See Brood Bitch.

Matted: See Felted.

Meat Hound: A hunting dog who can be relied upon to find game.

Member Show: A show recognized by the AKC.

Merle: A blue-grey coat marbled with black. Seen in Collies and Shetland Sheepdogs.

Merry Tail: A tail that is held high and wagged a great deal.

Middle Piece: Portion of the body between the shoulders and the hindquarters.

Milk/ Puppy Teeth: A pup's first set of teeth, which are replaced by the second (or permanent) set.

Mongrel: A dog who is a mixture of many different breeds.

Monorchid: A male dog with a testicle that has not descended into the scrotum. A fault.

Mops: Long, thick hair on all four paws.

Mutant: A dog whose traits vary from his breed. He has the ability to pass along such changed characteristics to his or her offspring.

Muzzle:
1. The part of the face consisting of the dog's nose and mouth.
2. A device made of leather strapping that covers the dog's mouth and nose, preventing him from eating and biting.

Neuter: See Alter.

Noseband: An area of white fur that completely surrounds the dog's nose and mouth. Seen in St. Bernards.

Novice Class: A show for dogs who have never won an adult dog show. (They may have won in the Puppy class.)

Obedience Trials: Obedience tests where dogs are put through certain exercises and scored by judges.

Occiput: A spot on the upper, back portion of the skull, which is prominent in some breeds. Seen in dogs of the Hound family.

Outbred: Mating of unrelated dogs of the same breed.

Overshot: A mouth with an upper jaw that protrudes beyond the lower jaw, causing the front teeth not to meet properly.

p.: Abbreviation for "puppy" in pedigrees and catalogues. It refers to a dog who is under one year of age.

Pack: A group of dogs who run together.

Pad: The cushioned part of a dog's foot.

Parasites: Minute organisms which live on, or inside, and at expense of the body of the dog. Those that infest a dog's coat are fleas, ticks, and lice. There is a tremendous variety of parasites.

Parti-Color: A coat description of fur that has two or more distinct colors in nearly equal proportion.

Pastern: The lowest part of the leg between the knee and foot, similar to the wrist in a human.

Paw: The dog's foot.

Pedigree: An official written record of a dog's ancestors, his owners, and breeders.

Piebald: A coat of two colors, with irregular patches of each, covering the body.

Pigmentation: Coloration usually referring to the darkness of toenails, rims of eyes, and nose.

Plucking: Removal of dead or unwanted hair from a dog's coat. Performed on Terriers.

Pooper-Scooper Law: A regulation that requires an owner to clean up after his dog defecates in the street.

Pricked Ears: Stiff and erect ears. Seen in Scottish Terriers, Chow Chows, Welsh Corgis.

Proven: A male or female dog who has parented one or more litters.

Put Down/ Put to Sleep/ Euthanasia: Refers to a dog being put to death painlessly.

Quick: The fleshly portion at the bottom of each claw.

Red: A reddish-brown coat.

Registration: The process of listing the pedigree and other pertinent information about a dog to prove that he or she is a pure strain.

Reserve Winner: A dog who places fourth in a competition.

Ring Tail: Tail carried up and around, almost making a complete circle.

Roan: A coat which is a mixture of white and another color (usually blue or red) in fairly equal proportions. Seen in Cocker Spaniels who are orange-roan, liver-roan, or blue-roan.

Rose Ear: An ear that folds backward, showing part of the inside. Seen in Bulldogs.

Ruff: A great deal of hair that forms a stand-up collar around the neck of a dog. Seen in Chow Chows and Collies.

Runt: An undersized pup who is the smallest in the litter.

Scapula: The shoulder blade.

Screw Tail: A short, twisted tail. Seen in Bulldogs.

Semiprick Ears: Ears that are erect but have the tips pointing down and forward. Seen in Collies.

Septum: The bone that separates the nostrils.

Shoulders: The largest bones beneath the level of the neck.

Sickle Tail: A long tail carried up and over the back in a semicircle. Seen in Spitz breeds.

Sire: The male parent of a pup.

Sled Dogs: Any of the breeds—for instance, Samoyed, Siberian Husky, Alaskan Malamute and Eskimo Dog—used to pull sleds in icy, snowy areas.

Snipy Muzzle: A pointed, weak muzzle.

Spay: To surgically remove the reproduction organs of a bitch.

Specials Only: A category in a dog show that allows only Champions to compete.

Spectacles: Dark markings around the eyes. Seen in Keeshonds.

Splay Feet: Paws that have spread-out toes. Seen in some sporting breeds.

Squirrel Tail: A short tail that curves over the back.

Stifle: The joint in the hind leg roughly equivalent to a human knee.

Stop: A dip between the foreface and forehead.

Stud: A male dog used for breeding purposes. (A fee is usually charged for his mating services.)

Tallyho: A hunting term which means "game in sight."

Tassels: Unclipped, long hair that remains on the ears of a dog as part of the style of his clip. Seen in Bedlington Terriers.

Tender-Mouthed: Able to carry game without tearing its skin. Seen in Retrievers.

Thorax: Chest.

Tricolor: Three-colored coat, usually black, white, and tan, in reasonably equal proportions.

Topknot: Long, fine hair on top of a dog's head. Seen in Dandie Dinmonts.

Topline: When the dog is seen in profile. This is an imaginary line from the top of the head to the base of the tail.

Trousers: Shaggy, long hair on the legs. Seen in Afghan Hounds.

Tulip Ears: Erect ears that slant forward slightly.

Undershot: Refers to a dog's jaw when the lower front teeth project beyond the upper ones.

Upper Arm: The section of the front leg between the elbow and the shoulder blade.

Varmint Expression: A beady-eyed expression. Seen in Terrier breeds.

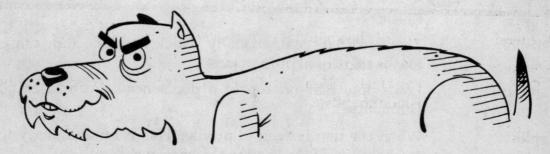

Vent: A patch of light-colored hair under the tail. (Also sometimes refers to the rectum.)

Vermin Dog: A dog who is good at killing rats and mice.

Walleye: An eye that is either totally blue, or blue with flecks of brown or black in the iris. Seen in Blue Merle Collies and some Great Danes.

Wheaten: A light fawn, or creamy-yellow color.

Whelping: Giving birth to puppies.

Whiptail: A long, straight, tapering tail. Seen in Pointers.

Whiskers: Stiff, long, single hairs on the front of the face and jaws.

Withers: Top of the shoulders where the neck joins the body.

Wrinkles: Loose folds of skin that pucker up the brow and sides of the face. Seen in Basenjis, Pugs, St. Bernards, and Bloodhounds.

Appendix:

- **Parts of a Dog**
- **Skeletal Structure**
- **Internal Organs**
- **Facial Types**
- **Jaw Variations**
- **Ear Variations**
- **Tail Variations**
- **Foot Variations**
- **The Breeds**

Parts of a Dog

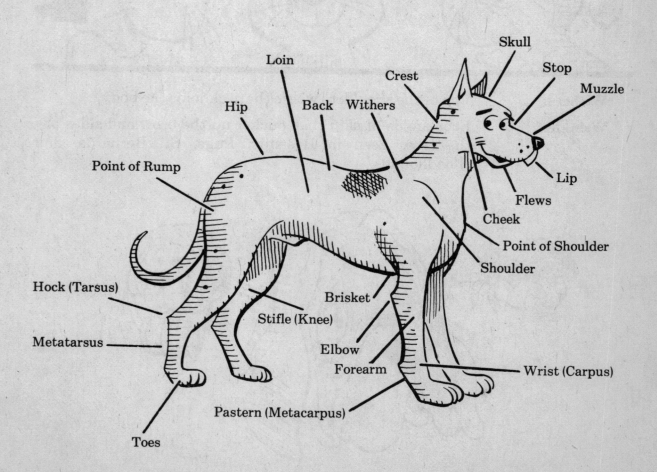

Skeleton

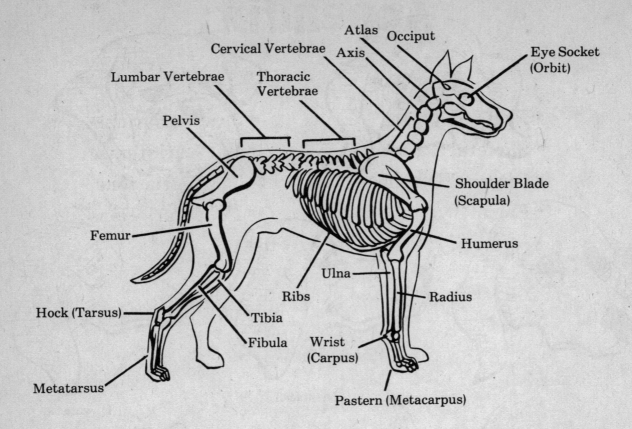

Internal Organs

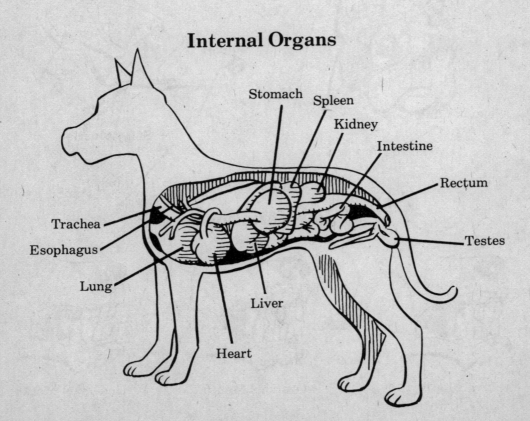

Facial Types

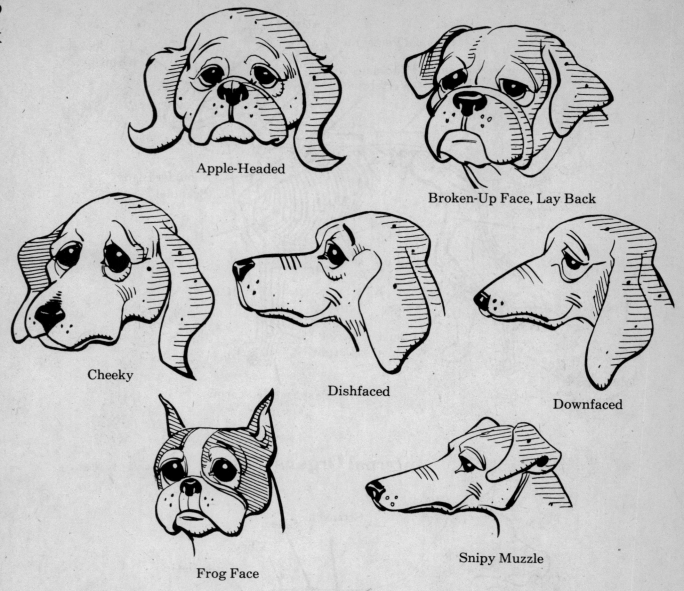

Apple-Headed

Broken-Up Face, Lay Back

Cheeky

Dishfaced

Downfaced

Frog Face

Snipy Muzzle

Jaw Variations

Level Mouth

Overshot Mouth

Undershot Mouth

Ear Variations

Bat Ear

Button Ear

Drop Ear

Prick Ear

Rose Ear

Semiprick Ear

Tail Variations

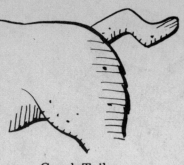

Crank Tail

Docked Tail

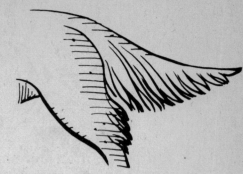

Feathered Tail

Gay Tail

Ring Tail

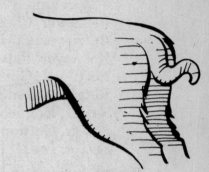

Screw Tail

Sickle Tail

Squirrel Tail

Whiptail

Foot Variations

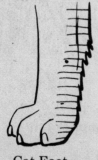

Cat Foot

Hare Foot

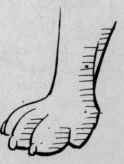

Splay Foot

The Breeds

Group I: SPORTING DOGS

Pointer
Pointer, German
    Shorthaired
Pointer, German
    Wirehaired
Retriever, Chesapeake Bay
Retriever, Curly-Coated
Retriever, Flat-Coated
Retriever, Golden
Retriever, Labrador
Setter, English
Setter, Gordon
Setter, Irish
Spaniel, American Water
Spaniel, Brittany
Spaniel, Clumber
Spaniel, Cocker

Spaniel, English Cocker
Spaniel, English Springer
Spaniel, Field
Spaniel, Irish Water
Spaniel, Sussex
Spaniel, Welsh Springer
Vizsla
Weimaraner
Wirehaired Pointing
    Griffon

Group II: HOUNDS

Afghan Hound
Basenji
Basset Hound
Beagle
Black and Tan
    Coonhound
Bloodhound

continued

Borzoi
Dachshund
Foxhound, American
Foxhound, English
Greyhound
Harrier
Ibizan Hound

Irish Wolfhound
Norwegian Elkhound
Otter Hound
Rhodesian Ridgeback
Saluki
Scottish Deerhound
Whippet

Group III: WORKING DOGS

Akita
Alaskan Malamute
Bearded Collie
Belgian Malinois
Belgian Sheepdog
Belgian Tervuren
Bernese Mountain Dog
Bouvier des Flandres
Boxer
Briard
Bullmastiff
Collie

Doberman Pinscher
German Shepherd Dog

Giant Schnauzer
Great Dane

Great Pyrenees
Komondor
Kuvasz
Mastiff
Newfoundland
Old English Sheepdog
Puli
Rottweiler
St. Bernard
Samoyed
Shetland Sheepdog
Siberian Husky
Standard Schnauzer
Welsh Corgi, Cardigan
Welsh Corgi, Pembroke

Group IV: TERRIERS

Airedale Terrier
American Staffordshire
  Terrier
Australian Terrier
Bedlington Terrier
Border Terrier
Bull Terrier
Cairn Terrier
Dandie Dinmont Terrier
Fox Terrier
Irish Terrier
Kerry Blue Terrier
Lakeland Terrier
Manchester Terrier
Miniature Schnauzer
Norfolk Terrier
Norwich Terrier
Scottish Terrier
Sealyham Terrier
Skye Terrier
Soft-Coated Wheaten
  Terrier

Staffordshire Bull
  Terrier
Welsh Terrier
West Highland White
  Terrier

Group V: TOYS

Affenpinscher
Brussels Griffon
Chihuahua
English Toy Spaniel
Italian Greyhound
Japanese Chin
Maltese
Manchester Terrier (Toy)
Miniature Pinscher
Papillon

continued

Pekinese
Pomeranian

Poodle (Toy)
Pug
Shih Tzu
Silky Terrier
Yorkshire Terrier

Group VI: NON-SPORTING DOGS

Bichon Frise
Boston Terrier
Bulldog

French Bulldog
Keeshond
Lhasa Apso
Poodle

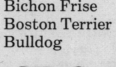

Chow Chow
Dalmatian

Schipperke
Tibetan Terrier